P9-EEP-152

Advanced Hockey for Women

Advanced Hockey for Women

BRENDA READ
& FREDA WALKER

FABER & FABER
3 Queen Square, London

First published in 1976
by Faber and Faber Limited
3 Queen Square London WC1N 3AU
Printed in Great Britain by
Latimer Trend & Company Ltd Plymouth
All rights reserved

ISBN 0 571 09881 9

CAMROSE LUTHERAN COLLEGE
LIBRARY

GV
1017
.H7
R4

21,683

© *1976 by Brenda Read and Freda Walker*

Contents

Illustrations

KEY TO LINE DRAWINGS

⟶ Movement of player

- - - - - - - - - - -▶ Movement of ball

▬ ▬ ▬ ▬ ▬ ▬ ▬ ▬▶ Movement of player with ball

Acknowledgements

OUR GRATEFUL THANKS are due to Miss Joyce Whitehead, Editor of the *Hockey Field,* who willingly allowed us to select much of our photographic material from her stock; to the Sports Council for supplying other photographs; and to the many people at Neville's Cross College and elsewhere who gave their time and expertise to assist in the typing of the script and the preparation of other photographic material. Their help was invaluable.

Foreword

Advanced Hockey for Women appears at an opportune moment, at a time when important changes have been made in the Rules of the Game, when new patterns of play have been introduced and when the established method of coaching is being critically examined.

Hockey is a fast-moving and exciting game, requiring quick thinking as well as physical skills. It gives pleasure to players and spectators alike; and the greater the skill, the greater the pleasure. Greater skill through expert coaching is the aim of the book.

The two authors, Brenda Read and Freda Walker, have wide experience in the game. Both have represented England as players; both are internationally renowned as coaches whose services are in demand at home and overseas. They are forward-thinking, introducing the best of new ideas into their coaching but at the same time they stress the need for basic skills, without which it is impossible to carry out the various tactics and patterns of play.

This book will be invaluable to all who coach hockey, making available as it does the expert knowledge gathered from years of successful coaching and, equally important, giving practical guidance as to 'how' and 'when'. It will also benefit the aspiring player, particularly in the sphere of tactical thinking, so necessary in outwitting opponents and in the setting up of attacking moves.

It is with confidence that I recommend this book to those who aim at higher levels of performance, whether as coaches or players, and thus at greater enjoyment in and from the game.

DORIS CRISP

President
All England Women's Hockey Association

1. Basic and Advanced Play

THIS BOOK IS intended for those who already appreciate the skills needed for playing good hockey, and have an understanding of the whole game. There are, of course, as many ways of coaching hockey as there are coaches, but we have a deep conviction that coaching should not be restricting for players; rather it should give opportunities for individuality to flourish without destroying team play. If the coach finds coaching pleasurable and stimulating, then her attitude will be contagious. At all costs we feel that solemnity should be avoided and seriousness stressed. Hockey is a mental and physical challenge and as such needs to be taken seriously, but not to such an extent that a sense of perspective is lost and the whole business becomes a burden. What is a game of hockey but an opportunity to combine intelligence, speed of judgement, speed of physical and mental reaction and expertise with stick and ball?

The Basic Game

Before we come to advanced play a brief look at more basic play will be valuable.

In a basic game one is hoping to see some semblance of regular organized formation so that all players in a team have some security. They can expect certain people to be in a certain area at a certain time. For example, when the play is in the left side of the defending circle, the defending team can expect the left wing and the left inner to be close enough to collect a short, quick pass. Such organization gives players more freedom to assess and deal with opponents singly or in groups. At this stage, as at all stages, good footwork and good, accurate stickwork need to be present. A wide range of stickwork is

not essential but what is known must be well executed and capable
of variation in timing and pace. For example, seldom will there be
time for a hard drive in copy-book style, with well-balanced backlift
and follow-through, weight on the left foot and with the ball
exactly the right distance from the feet.

A player must be able to drive short or long distances at a pace
suitable to the occasion, drive from either foot and shorten the
length of time taken for backlift and follow-through. Each player
needs to know the minimum of two ways of sending a ball, of
keeping possession and of taking possession. Otherwise, the opposition will know in advance what she is about to do. At any level of
play that state of affairs reduces the game to an ordeal of patience
and fortitude.

Accuracy of placing as well as timing, both of which presuppose
that a sound judgement has been made, is essential to the most basic
game. A back who hits the ball hard is an asset only so long as that
hit sends the ball to or for one of her own players. The back who
glories in the power of her hit rather than its purpose may become
an asset to the opposition because the ball goes out of play or goes
to or for her opponents.

Even at this stage, time and space are at a premium. Lack of
individual skill will make sending the ball or carrying the ball a
relatively slow process, whereas tackling is not necessarily slower
because it is begun without having to control the ball. Whenever
the movement of the ball is ponderous the spaces through which
the ball might travel seem to diminish or disappear with the speed
of light. We all know that left wing, just learning her job, who takes
5 yd. (4·57 m.) of running to move the ball to her right, 7 yd.
(6·4 m.) of running to get her feet ahead of the ball and 3 yd.
(2·74 m.) of running backwards to lift and drop her stick in order to
centre. By this time the goal-line is imminent and there is too little
space in the circle for even the smallest ball to pass through.

The Advanced Game

Advanced play is not necessarily the outcome of a match employing
advanced players, nor does it necessarily produce a more complex
game. Much that is seen in a basic game will be seen here too.

Often the speed and finesse of execution may lead one to reject the thought that these could be the same tactics and techniques seen in a game of lesser calibre and yet it is simplicity augmented that forms the basis of advanced play. For us, the latter is more than a display of expertise. It reveals a constant buoyancy; a positive probing for and using of information; spontaneity; individual sparkle and group cohesion. From the start there is an obvious air of organization; speed of movement of the players and ball that delights the eye; easy flow of play; assurance in the stickwork, fast and effective footwork; an acute sense of timing of the dodging player who moves the ball when her opponent is a breath away; the accuracy of a pass that is just incapable of being intercepted, but tempts the opponent into committing herself utterly. Every player is eager for the ball. This is it, that myth, the advanced game —a highly mobile form of chess where every movement and every thought from every player is geared to making the opposition look and feel like beginners, giving the impression that their play is dictated even when they have the ball. Consciousness of colleagues and self, though still important, comes second and third in importance to awareness of the opposition. The game is now at its simplest and most advanced level. Simple to describe because it is merely a practical experience of seeing, creating and using space; advanced because doing the latter requires such speed of physical and mental reaction and such technical expertise. Of the many factors which are combined for advanced play to be achieved, the most essential is the interaction of the twenty-two players and their attitude to the particular game. For instance, many international matches produce disappointing play because the importance of the occasion creates intensity which can submerge the players' resilience.

The Coach

In the same way that advanced players need to use and also refine basic skills and tactics, so the advanced coach should always keep elementary coaching methods in mind as a basis for her work. From these she can invent, develop, adapt to meet the increased demands of coaching highly skilled players.

The personal qualities of the coach are of vital importance. In particular she needs the ability to create an atmosphere of easy rapport within a context of mutual respect. Any individual undertaking the task of coaching must be convinced that she has something of value to offer to the players she is to meet. A sense of humour may well be an easy way of making quick contact and reducing the excess tension that can sometimes exist at coaching sessions. Experience of, and contact with, high-level play will be an advantage to the coach, for she needs to sustain a constant flow of up-to-date ideas. Provided she is open-minded to the suggestions of those she is coaching, prepared to be absolutely truthful in her comments and ready to admit openly to being wrong, there is a fair chance that positive improvements can come from the encounter. Being in any position of authority brings in its train some isolation and attracts adverse criticism. A good coach will be prepared to take this in her stride and learn from it whenever possible.

We realize that coaching is a controversial issue. In the current climate of games playing there seem to be two strongly opposed views; the one which maintains that much more intensive coaching is needed, and the other which believes coaching merely produces stereotyped play and should be avoided. Each could be valid in certain circumstances depending on the calibre of coach, of the players and on the general conditions surrounding the situation. Having benefited ourselves from good coaching we believe it to be of great value.

In this book we put before the reader a collection of our experiences as players and coaches in the hope that we may offer ideas to stimulate thoughts on coaching, inspire would-be international players and provoke constructive discussion.

2. *Stick to Practising*

Advanced Skills

OBSERVATION OF A top-level game will reveal diversity of style and a wide range of stickwork, usually built up through years of practice and experimentation. Individuals can be seen to vary from a rigidly functional approach to the other extreme of sheer artistry. The final style which an individual evolves is influenced by the basic teaching received; her physical attributes and deficiencies; whether or not she has tried to emulate another player; and her desire to continue perfecting her skill for its own sake. Real mastery only develops when a player is not only motivated by the need to be effective, but also by an aesthetic appreciation of the skills under her control.

Skills should be so well learned that they can survive pressure and retain their effectiveness. There is a tendency for players who are pressured to resort to those skills in which they have greatest confidence. They become less willing to take risks and this limited approach to the game makes their play more predictable and more easily counteracted. Observation will also reinforce the point that the real experts are more consistent and their skill can withstand the pressure of increased competition, unlike lesser performers who find this more difficult. It is a great asset for a player to be confident in her own ability even when those around her are lapsing into mediocrity.

In hockey we are concerned not only with skilled actions but also the way in which these skills are applied. Skill involves, therefore, not only technical expertise, but also the ability to adapt one's responses and assess beforehand the needs of the situation. The player may need to release the ball immediately on receiving it or maintain possession while creating or waiting for a more suitable moment. Thus decision-making becomes important because the player needs to pay attention to the picture of the whole game, make rapid judgements, select the appropriate response and then act. It is obviously an advantage to be able to select a response from a wide repertoire in order to meet the demands of the situation as accurately as possible.

Skill is functional in that it is designed and produced to achieve a known objective, and the success of that skilled action is determined by how nearly the original intention is achieved. For example, success in placing a pass is judged by how closely it approaches the target. Thus if we accept that skilled actions in hockey are purposeful and goal-directed, and not merely expressive, we can also categorize these skills and assess them objectively in terms of success or failure.

If skills are to be goal-directed, they must be related to tactics. Remember tactics are present as soon as an individual player matches her skill against an opponent and the successful exploitation of any tactical situation depends on good reading of the game and the ability to perform the skills which are necessary to achieve the tactical objective. It is important to understand the interpretation given to the word 'skill'. Skill involves the peculiar abilities of each player, linked with good timing and the appropriate application of techniques to the game. Techniques, on the other hand, are specific skilled actions. The drive is a good example where the combination of footwork and the manipulation of the stick and ball produces a pattern which is easily recognizable.

Techniques can be executed in isolation (for example, a free hit) or they can be part of a sequence of actions where the effectiveness of each succeeding action depends upon what has gone before (for example, a dodge round a defender followed by a shot). Accumulated errors in such a sequence call for greater adaptation and consequently higher levels of skill. The good player who can, by her skill in receiving, make a bad pass look good is a prize example.

Each player is endowed with certain abilities which affect the level of proficiency attainable. Players develop attitudes towards skills which influence their approach to the game. Young players who are currently finding their way into selected teams, by their approach to the game, advertise the way they have been taught and the types of pitch on which they acquired their technical expertise.

Those who have developed on a fast, artificial surface frequently display delicacy of stick control, but all too often they approach the ball with the intention to push, when a drive would be more suitable. A habit forms, and their game lacks the power which is so essential at times.

Another factor which can affect the proficiency of a player is the choice of stick. Acquisition of hockey techniques can be made easier by using a stick which is of suitable size and weight. Contrary to popular belief a heavier stick does not necessarily increase the power of the drive since the speed of the swing is more influential. A player with a lighter stick does not need to work so hard on the swing itself nor does she need to carry the extra weight, sometimes in one hand, for the seventy minutes of the game; hence, a lower expenditure of energy. A longer stick should not be chosen with the claim that it extends the reach of the player. Good footwork should solve that problem. A thick handle in relation to the hand size is not advisable as it tends to produce rigidity in the wrists, and this prevents the stick from twisting in the hands, which in turn makes manipulation of the head of the stick more difficult. Ideally the fingers should be able to close around the handle. Dexterity is essential. If the head of the stick is too thick it can restrict the ability to lift balls in the scoop, flick or fling strokes.

The game of hockey makes two demands with regard to skill: namely, consistency and adaptability. Hitting a stationary ball at a corner to an exact spot requires the former. This can be practised quite easily as the objective is clear. Success is easily measurable and it is appropriate that the action becomes almost automatic so that it can be repeated exactly on future occasions. After regular practice by many players a corner-hitting expert may emerge to take over the role habitually given to wing players. In this way an individual's specific skill may be used to the mutual advantage of the whole team.

Superb timing is one of the hallmarks of the highly skilled performer for even if a player anticipates another's intentions, accurate timing is still needed for the skill to be effective. A player's thoughts and actions must be in harmony in the same way that her skill must match the speed of her ability to make decisions in circumstances where speed is vital. The ability to read the game quickly may enable a player to have more time to respond in some circum-

stances, thereby giving the impression of being unhurried. One
factor very evident in good players is alertness: that acute interest in
all that happens around them. Reading the game is made easier
when a player is highly skilled for she is able to withdraw her conscious awareness from the actual execution of the stroke and focus
it on changes occurring during the game.

Returning to the observation of a top-class game, it is evident
that skilled performance displays economy of effort, quicker
responses, greater accuracy, fluency and the impression of having
plenty of time to deal with the situation. Combining alertness,
knowledge of the game and skill, a player is rarely caught unawares.
This may be one reason why spectators following some top-level
games are heard to express disappointment at the lack of flair or to
proclaim the game dull. In highly skilled games it is likely that there
will be fewer surprises because everybody is reading the game well
in advance, is prepared for what is to come and is equipped to deal
with it. There is a levelling out of ability which means that one
player can rarely show superiority over another. In a closely
matched game, attacking breakthroughs tend to be a direct result of
errors on the part of the defenders. A good player in a lower-level
game can beat a number of players at will, but when matched
against those of equal ability and experience she has to do much
more to be successful. It is vital that she is prepared mentally and
physically to meet such a challenge. Thus, when learning techniques
it is essential to acquire them in a way that is closely related to the
game and at the maximum controlled speed.

Fitness is an essential part of the game. Techniques deteriorate
as fatigue increases so players must work to improve their strength,
speed and stamina. Many games are won or lost in the final minutes
and it would be tragic to lose a game because players were too unfit
to perform the skills they have practised so long. Fitness is specific
to each individual but most players need to add activities to their
training which will help their bodies to meet the demands to be
made on them. Carefully planned practice sessions with stick and
ball can go a long way towards producing the required level of
fitness and it is advisable, using pressure practices, to combine
stickwork with fitness training.

Practice Methods

'Practice' can be defined as any activity which a player undertakes in order to try to modify or consolidate skilled actions. Simple repetition of an action is not enough, for all practice should stress quality. Quantity alone is not sufficient, and indeed the practice of wrong movements may only serve to confirm bad habits and so be detrimental. Normally it is accepted that shorter, more frequent practice sessions are most beneficial, but if the criterion of quality is applied, then it can be seen that length and distribution of practice sessions will be determined by how much a player can absorb and how long she can sustain the standard of the practice.

Different procedures may be adopted according to the objectives of the coaching session and the ability of the players taking part. Basically three situations emerge.

The first of these arises when the players are able to produce a recognizable version of the whole technique immediately after attending to instructions and seeing a visual demonstration, and are able to modify subsequent repetitions to eliminate any faults present in the initial attempt. This is really only possible where the skills involved are fairly simple or well within the scope of the players concerned. When observing the efforts made it is important for the coach to be able to differentiate between the desirable elements of a skilled performance and those elements which will detract from efficiency. This method of working on the whole action should be adopted where possible because it allows maximum activity and, providing it falls within the ability range of the players it takes less time to produce an acceptable version of the technique. Points of technique need not be explained to the players once they have seen the picture of the whole action as it is sufficient to allow them to copy the demonstration and then evaluate the results. Then the coach and the player can identify faults which recur over the first few attempts. Remember the initial effort is rarely typical and do not fall into the trap of making your diagnosis too early. Individual remedies then need to be provided. When a large group is involved the most common faults will need to be identified and coped with first while the few individuals who are encountering particular problems are dealt with separately. Where more than one fault exists these should be ranked in priority order and the most basic one dealt with first since the correction of one fault may contribute to the elimination of others.

The second situation is one in which the players have achieved a reasonable level of competence, but where faults persist. As the fault cannot be eliminated through repeating the whole action it is necessary to isolate the fault and employ a corrective practice. When this is successful the modified part is absorbed into the whole action. For example, in the fling stroke a player may be getting lift and length, but insufficient spin because of poor wrist action. The player can slow the whole action down by placing the head of the stick underneath the ball and by lifting the ball higher initially while effecting the correct wrist action.

Success or failure can be assessed by noting the reaction of the ball in flight (facilitated by using a ball painted half-black and half-white) and also its reaction against the ground. The practice is made easier by removing the power required to gain length, and reintroducing it later. If success is not realized it may be necessary for further corrective measures to be applied. A discerning coach may speed up the learning process by more skilful analysis which enables her to select the most appropriate procedure from a pool of corrective measures. The coach needs to have a number of different remedies at her fingertips to suit the needs of individual players. Really individual coaching is essential here because of shortage of time and the need for close guidance throughout the practice period. Frequently players who are already fairly competent are reluctant to work on minor discrepancies and they need to see the long-term benefits to be gained if they are to be motivated to make a real effort.

The third situation is one in which players are trying to acquire complex techniques which are too difficult for them to experience early success. It may be necessary to build up the technique in progressive stages where the skill is learnt as a series of interrelated actions which eventually combine to produce the whole action. Few isolated techniques in hockey are so complex as to demand this type of practice, but it is beneficial where isolated actions are linked together to produce a sequence of events, where additional problems are involved in mastering the transitions between the separate actions and where timing becomes particularly influential.

For example, a player may need to run to receive the ball and swerve as contact is made, followed by an immediate checking of the movement to reposition and shoot for goal. Receiving, swerving, checking and shooting can all be practised separately and then they are chained together in the correct order and the sequence progressively acquired.

Structuring Practices

Practices should be planned bearing the following points in mind:
(a) The simplest, clearest possible structure should be designed to achieve the required objective.
(b) Adequate space should be provided. Players cannot concentrate on the matter in hand if they are conscious of having to avoid other people.
(c) A realistic playing surface is advisable. The first attempt at any technique greatly influences future development. Therefore, it is unwise to learn to scoop off a hard surface or try to develop close dribbling at speed in thick mud and long grass.
(d) Ample equipment should be available so that time is not lost collecting balls, for example, when practising corner hitting.
(e) Practices should be orientated towards the normal direction of play when a pitch is being used.
(f) Optimum size of groups should be used to ensure maximum practice of the specific technique. For example, a player learning to fling a ball needs only a pile of balls and a fence. A player practising the double technique of 'receive and pass' can play the major role in a group of three. Player A feeds a ball to player B, who has to find moving target player C, who collects the ball. This is repeated and all three players are getting practice in passing and receiving, but only one player is combining the two actions. This is a rotation practice which means that the players move round to work in each of three positions following a given number of repetitions. It is advisable when structuring the size of groups to avoid moving from twos to threes because of the time taken to regroup. This can be speeded up, if it is necessary, by forming twos into sixes and then dividing the large group in half.

(g) Practices should be continuous or repeated after each attempt.

(h) The current ability of the players should be considered for this will largely determine the space they need, the amount of pressure which can be applied and the number of consecutive turns which can be expected before fatigue sets in. In more advanced coaching one can expect players to do much of this organization for themselves. The lower the level of ability the more detailed the organization needs to be.

Pressure Practices

These are used to simulate a harder situation than the one anticipated during the game, so that the actual event feels comparatively easy. Pressure can be applied through the restriction of time or space or both. Applying both restrictions is equivalent to the presence of opposition. Pressure practices can be designed for individuals and for groups. For example, when working as an individual, a player can use a wall as a partner. She can run parallel to it, driving the ball on to it at an angle, meeting it from the rebound, carrying it and driving again. A simple example of imposing pressure of time can be seen when two players each with a ball start simultaneously side by side and dribble in a race to a line 10 yd. (9·14 m.) away on which the ball must be stopped dead.

Pressure practices frequently involve putting a player in the hot seat and the following example illustrates this. Three players are involved. Players A and B each have a ball. Player C is positioned about 10 yd. (9·14 m.) in front of them. A drives the ball straight ahead of herself, C moves sideways to collect it and returns it to A. Player B drives her ball straight ahead of herself whilst C is recovering to her central position. C meets this ball and returns it to B before immediately recovering to meet the second drive from player A. This is repeated for as long as player C can keep the practice going. The receiver should aim to run with her shoulders facing the feeders all the time. Time pressure can be increased by strengthening the drive, by increasing the sideways distance the receiver has to cover, by shortening the distance between the receiver and the feeders or by the feeders releasing the ball earlier. The drive, fling or push strokes can be used in this practice. The final example is devised around a restriction of space. Confined to an area 4 yd. (3·66 m.) square two players are given possession of the ball and an opponent introduced who attempts to get the ball. The two players must keep the ball within the square and are allowed to pass or dodge in order to avoid the opponent. They are not allowed to break any rules applicable in the full game of hockey.

Pressure practices are designed to be physically demanding as well as exacting in terms of the skill required to make them work effectively. They should be interspersed with less vigorous activities if players are to derive maximum benefit from them.

A coach frequently faces a dilemma when coaching experienced players. Namely, whether or not to try to strengthen a player's technical weaknesses or consolidate on her strengths. It is evident that in working on the weaknesses, the strengths can deteriorate and so it may be more beneficial to structure the team tactics to make the most of her strengths and hide her weaknesses. It is well known that old habits die hard and a great deal of time is required if skills are to be broken down and restructured to advantage.

The following guidelines might be worthy of attention in the coaching of techniques:

(a) Cover a wide range of skills as early as possible. The ease or difficulty of different techniques must be related to each player and it is likely that there will be personal differences. Do not tell a player that a skill is difficult before she attempts it, and remember that mastery of difficult skills may make simpler skills easier to learn.

(b) In addition to the visual information which is available to the performer the coach must provide criticism to enable a player to make accurate adjustments both prior to and during the repetition of an action. For example a player may see her drive fail to reach its target. She can see the results of her efforts, but she may not know why the ball went astray. This is where the coach can provide a verbal comment such as 'keep the left shoulder pointing towards the target until the stroke is completed.' This can be reinforced during the next attempt by the coach instructing the player as she repeats the action and in helping her with the timing. Later attempts may only require the word 'shoulder' as a reminder before leaving the player to consolidate the corrected action.

(c) Incentives for success such as selection for a national team may already exist and motivation must be moderated accordingly. A player already concerned about her ability to make the grade may become over-anxious if motivated too strongly, resulting in deterioration of performance.

(d) Initially, techniques may be learnt in isolation, especially if they are complex and if the player already shows some lack of confidence in the game, but as soon as possible practice should become realistic and applied directly to the game. It is essential for a player to learn not only the technique but how her execution of it fits into the whole pattern of the game.

(e) Once the pattern of the action is established it should be speeded up to the maximum controlled speed which can be coped with by each individual.

(f) Because hockey skills are perceptual, in that they are displayed in response to stimuli from the game, the players need to learn how to search the game for information and this necessitates their attention being drawn from the actual execution of the technique on occasions. This is only possible if the skills are so well learnt that they can be done without the need for conscious control.

(g) Only the most important information should be given to a learner before she has a go. She needs to have a mental picture of the finished product and to understand what it is designed to achieve, and she needs to receive only one or two points on which she can concentrate while practising.

(h) When an error is made, the player should not be allowed to repeat this or it may become established. Some modification must occur, based on information offered by the coach or collected by the player herself on the evidence of the results of the action.

(i) Where a player finds difficulty in complying with an instruction from a coach it is sometimes beneficial to draw the attention of the learner away from her own feeling of whether or not she is doing the right thing and towards structuring the environment so that only the right action can be completed. For example, use the proximity of a wall to restrict the size of the backlift in the drive.

(j) Speed and accuracy are interrelated. It is important to decide

whether speed or accuracy should receive most stress when learning a skill. Where speed is essential to the success of the action
then it is unwise to practise that skill slowly, but where accuracy
is crucial, practice at a slower pace can be more beneficial for a
time, knowing that it is not always possible to take time to be
careful during the game.

One of the difficulties of coaching techniques is that they are
governed by an adherence to certain principles in order to be
effective. Good style, instead of being the product of the personal
expression of those principles, is thought by some to be merely the
decoration on the cake. Good style involves doing the basic actions
well with economy of effort and it is largely enhanced by perfect
timing. Individual preferences for range and speed of movement
establish the style of each player. Every player is free to express her
skills in her own way, but the unnecessary flourish with the stick or
some idiosyncrasy of footwork or posture can, at top level, be a
disadvantage if these advertise the intentions of the player, especially where deception is required. On the other hand, much interest
would be lost from the game if such variations in style were smoth-
ered. Individuality and flair are to be encouraged providing they are
constructed on the basic framework which will offer the best chance
of success.

Techniques, then, are developed to enable players to use tactics
and so, as well as being proficient in a wide range of skills, each
individual will also develop a personal repertoire of skills which are
peculiar to her playing position and the role she is expected to play
in the team, and which suit her strengths and weaknesses.

Here are four examples. A left half back has to be able to tackle
from the non-stick side in order to keep between her opponent and
the goal. She may opt for any of the following methods: one, a jab
tackle; two, a circular tackle; three, a one-handed reverse stick
tackle; four, a two-handed reverse stick tackle. She is able to choose
her angle of approach and the choice of tackle may be largely determined by her speed in relation to that of her opponent, or the
strength of her left wrist. Thus, although a choice of methods is
available, the final choice is determined by the needs of the situation,
the abilities and preferences of the players concerned, and by the
movement which is to follow the successful completion of the
tackle. A centre-forward needs to develop especially close ball

control in a confined space in addition to immediate and effective
changes of pace and the ability to dribble fairly long distances
at high speed. Defenders frequently need to control and clear the
ball with as little hesitation as possible.

The position into which a player settles should reflect the majority of her strengths, although she is likely to have some weaknesses
which need to be hidden or improved. An established right wing
who finds difficulty in hitting hard to the right as she rarely has to
use it, may avoid interchanging to a large extent. Such specializa-
tion in positional play is limiting and may hinder a player's advance-
ment as she cannot be used elsewhere.

Analysis of Techniques

The techniques will be considered in detail according to their
function and methods of practice. The following principles under-
lie all the strokes and a concentration on these will help in the
development of an effective technique:
(a) the importance of footwork before, during and after the stroke;
(b) utilization of power from the legs and hips when maximum
    force is required;
(c) keeping the head over the ball at the moment of contact;
(d) a compact preparation which retains control of the head of the
    stick;
(e) a follow-through to aid fluency, help maintain power and direc-
    tion;
(f) use of a suitable grip which varies with the stroke and to some
    extent with individual preferences.

Travelling with the Ball

Dribbling is used to enable a player to cover ground with the ball
in her possession, as a preparation for other strokes—for example,
when manoeuvring to pass or shoot, to move away from an attempted
tackle, or to accelerate into a space and so draw a defender away
from a crowded area.

The techniques required vary according to the needs of the
situation. Normally we encourage players to concentrate on main-

taining close control where the ball is kept on the stick and steered in the desired direction. This push dribble necessitates continuous contact with the ball which is essential when moving in confined spaces. However, if a player is less pressured and wishes to cover ground more quickly, then contact with the ball is likely to be more spasmodic, especially when the playing surface is poor. Indeed, when there is a clear space ahead the ball may be deliberately hit forward, chased and collected, as a player without the ball can travel faster than a player with the ball.

Four techniques for dribbling should be considered. Players on the left of the field anticipating the need to pass right should acquire a 'drag' dribble whereby the feet run slightly ahead of the ball. This shortens the preparation required to pass right, enabling a player to disguise the intended pass more easily as it will be completed in a shorter time. The preparatory movements are reduced to a pivot of the feet and a twist in the body to bring the left shoulder round to point towards the target. Players on the right of the field anticipating the need to pass to the left should dribble the ball in front of the feet so that it can be guided quickly to the left foot before the pass is made. The ability to maintain close control while swerving in different directions is a prerequisite for evading opponents and is facilitated by dribbling with the ball in front of the feet allowing for an immediate movement to either side. This can be accomplished more easily by employing an alternate orthodox and reverse stick dribble where the ball travels on a zigzag. This is used mostly to confuse approaching defenders.

If a player is crouched too low over the stick, she will not be able to run freely and will limit the amount she can see. If players are taught to dribble with the hands apart on the stick there is a tendency for them to drop the right hand too low, so it may be better to start them dribbling with the hands together at the top of the stick and then encourage them to lower the right hand a few inches, until they feel they have better control. Do this while they are running as quickly as they can manage, then introduce swerving round obstacles, stopping and starting quickly, swerving round moving players in a confined space, and accelerating and decelerating without losing control.

Passing

The drive will be used in preference to any other stroke when it is necessary to send the ball long distances, to penetrate a rapidly closing gap or to meet a fast-moving player. The value of the drive lies in its versatility. Greatest power is achieved when the head is over the ball at impact, the stick is vertical and the left arm is an extension of the stick handle. A stick which is too long can cause a player to be cramped when the ball is ideally positioned close to the feet, or cause her to make room by pushing the ball further away, leading to a lateral swing of the stick from which the direction is more difficult to control. A high left shoulder over a braced leading leg will keep the ball on line and this is easy to achieve when the swing is in the vertical plane; as the swing becomes more circular excessive rotations are set up in the body which can cause off-balance and a consequent loss of accuracy.

Driving is a linear action. The hands are taken back away from the body in the opposite direction to the intended drive, the feet drive the body into the stroke and the left shoulder holds the swing on line to complete the follow-through. Force can only be applied to the ball during the period of contact which is very short and so the follow-through does not contribute to the speed of the ball, but it does maintain the line of action and aid a balanced recovery. The player should be concerned with the preparatory swing of the stick, which ideally should be short and fast. Because of the limits of stick height imposed by the rules, speed of swing is more important. By taking the hands away from the body the possibility of giving 'sticks' is largely eliminated. The wrists do bend upwards towards the completion of the downward swing and should be encouraged to do so since this whipping movement of the hands, bringing the head of the stick through late, greatly adds to the power of the stroke. At times it will be essential to drive as hard as possible, but most frequently passes require careful judgement of pace as well as direction, particularly when the ball has to be contained in a restricted area. Thus once a player has mastered the shape of the stroke it is important that she plays around with the idea of pace judgement.

Good footwork in the drive will be produced if all the principles mentioned previously are followed. If the feet are to force the hips into the stroke they must be close enough to allow the transfer of weight to take place and must point in the required direction and have a lively contact with the ground. Over the years certain players who appear to fly over the ground and readjust their position in a flash lodge in the memory because of their excellent footwork. Ursula Fairbairn and Angela Harrison, who were seen playing for South Africa against England at Wembley Stadium in 1965, were perfect examples of the art of neat footwork.

All these basic points apply to the drive whether it is from a standing position or on the run. Driving a dead ball is generally better accomplished if the ball is played off the left foot, but in the interests of deception a quick pass to the right may be aided by stepping through with the right foot. No such deception is needed when executing an accurate flat hit at a corner. Specialist methods can be used. The striker may stand sideways on to the ball like a golfer, placing both hands together some way down the handle in a 'chopper' grip. A short, crisp, firm swing from the shoulders can be effected or, alternatively, the swing of the stick can be produced entirely by the use of the wrists. In both cases there is no movement of the feet and the body is fairly rigid in order to aid the power and accuracy of the hit. The drive should be played off either foot with ease whether the player is moving slowly or at maximum speed. Too many players need to slow down before hitting. The drive to the left presents fewer difficulties because the left shoulder is already leading the way, but the ball needs to be positioned opposite the left foot to make things easier. Skilled players can execute a perfectly good flat drive to the left with the ball opposite the right foot. The weight is shifted over to that foot and the body is falling away to the right as the ball is struck. Difficult but deceptive, although occasionally resulting in some loss of power.

The drive to the right requires greater bodily adjustments in order to bring the left shoulder round to point in the direction of the intended pass. This brings about a twist in the body while the feet continue running forwards, the ball needs to be behind the rear foot so that the stick can swing freely behind the body. Immediately prior to impact the right foot thrusts through in the line of the hit to take the weight. This necessitates skilful balance and few players seem able to do this at speed. The pass to the right is so often advertised by the sluggish positioning of the feet, the loss of

B

impetus and the prolonged manoeuvre to get the ball in the right place. How frustrating it is to see so many players pull the ball back in order to pass to the right instead of relying on acceleration, twist in the body and dynamic balance.

So far we have suggested how a player can be ideally positioned to execute a drive, but in the game this happy state of affairs does not always exist. It is vital that a player can still make an effective drive when off balance, or having to cope with a bumpy or lush surface, or being pressured by an opponent or running out of space. The reverse stick drive can usefully be employed on occasion to meet such conditions to enable a player to pass to the right or backwards with fewer preliminary adjustments.

Reverse stick play applies whenever the stick is used with the toe of the head pointing in towards the player instead of away. Thus, if the ball is to the left of the player and the state of the game demands that she pass to the right, the stick is reversed, preferably with the toe being turned to the left, and the ball can be driven from left to right across the body. The same principles apply as in the normal drive although players who experience difficulty in swinging the stick this way may be helped by shortening their grip; that is, taking both hands lower down the handle or placing the hands slightly apart. When the hands are together the left hand predominates, working behind the stick, and if the hands are apart the right hand predominates by pulling the stick through. With the stick reversed the ball can also be passed backwards on the right-hand side of the body. Greater power is achieved if the full blade rather than just the toe of the stick meets the ball. Hence, the stick should be vertical.

The push stroke is used when attempting to deceive an opponent by not advertising the pass with a preparation of the stick—in other words when it is necessary to move the ball away quickly to avoid being tackled or to take advantage of an immediate and short-lived opportunity. As suggested, there is no preparation as the stick is in contact with the ball which is swept away using both hands in unison. The ball is placed level with the front foot and power is added by driving the hips into the stroke off the back foot. Although both hands work in the direction of the push, the left hand acts mainly as the fulcrum for the work of the right hand. To cover a longer distance or increase the speed of the stroke even further the ball can be placed opposite the rear foot, a more sideways stance adopted and the stick can be swept over a greater range. However, with this method the advantage of surprise is frequently lost as a wide base and a static stance normally precede the movement of the ball. Also the leverage is altered as the stick must start further from the body, while the left hand moves the top of the stick backwards before thrusting forwards and initiating the work from the right hand. The push is ideal on fast surfaces where it can be powerful and accurate. Control of pace is generally easier with the push than with the drive as contact with the ball is prolonged and more sensitive.

The fling stroke starts in the same way as the powerful push, but, as well as the contribution made by the body, power is gained by adding a last-minute flick of the wrists and the lift achieved by laying the head of the stick back underneath the ball before beginning the forward movement. This stroke should only be used as a pass when the ball is being sent into a space or the spin is turning the ball into the receiver to make close control possible. The stroke can be effected without lift and the ball flicked along the ground spinning as it goes. Either is useful for sending the ball between two opponents to make interception more difficult, and the presence of lift can avoid the disruptive influence of a bad playing surface. Flexibility and whip are the hallmarks of these strokes, and spin can be applied clockwise by wiping the blade of the stick underneath the ball, or anti-clockwise by wiping it up and over the top of the ball. With clockwise spin the ball will tend to hit the ground and kick to the right or hold a straight line, the converse being true when the spin is applied in the opposite direction. Thus when a left half or left inner is passing a forward ball to the left wing clockwise spin will reduce the risk of the ball rolling out of play over the side-line. When the ball is played directly to the stick of the left wing anti-clockwise spin will help her to trap the ball on the blade of the stick, as it will be moving towards her.

The scoop stroke is used when height is required as well as length, and this is normally a reverse stick technique in that the ball is played from the left-hand side of the body and the grip adjusted so that the stick is used like a shovel. Some players prefer to reverse their hands: that is, place the right hand at the top of the handle and the left hand lower down so that the stroke is made to the right of the body. In either case the handle of the stick is lowered to bring the stick from the vertical towards the horizontal with the blade facing upwards. The blade is inserted as far under the ball as possible to establish maximum contact and the body and stick are lifted together.

All these strokes can be used for shooting as well as for passing, but whereas the pass is designed to be easy to receive whenever the situation allows, the shot is used to send the ball past players into the goal. Because of the pressure situation normally pertaining in the circle, a player rarely has a chance to 'set the ball up' for a shot, is less likely to be ideally positioned to make the shot and yet must make every effort to produce an effective attempt at goal. This is where originality and flair can really show themselves, and this is one of the most challenging and exciting aspects of forward play. Generally, successful shots depend on the ball outpacing the opponents, the unexpectedness of the shot or its awkward placing. However, all forwards can remember the lucky goals scored because the ball took an unexpected bounce or deflection. It is most satisfying to score with a brilliant shot, but frequently a weak shot, although not directly effective, may provide a scoring opportunity for another player following up.

Receiving

In free play the prerequisite for a good pass is control of the moving ball coming in to a player. The ball can be hit first time so that the pass is really a redirection of the approaching ball, frequently with the addition of some pace to speed up the quick passing movement between two players used to eliminate an opponent or take immediate advantage of a diminishing space. When needing to collect the ball and hold it on the stick without fear of harassment, all players should be prepared to make space in order to receive it either by meeting the ball or dropping away from an opponent before the ball is passed. The full blade of the stick should be turned to face the approaching ball and the stick should be on the ground ready to lift and gather the ball which pops up unexpectedly. The stick should be considered to be a magnet attracting the ball to it and a relaxed grip will help to cushion the ball on impact and hold it in close to the stick. Lively footwork will make repositioning easier. It may help a player to try to watch the ball right on to the stick. To actually do so is extremely difficult, and in reasonable conditions the skilled player will have directed her attention elsewhere before contact is made.

When wishing to stop the ball dead, the right hand may be lowered down the handle to give close support to the blade of the stick as the ball is contacted. This more static method of receiving is used primarily at corners and by defenders fielding a hard ball coming straight towards them. Attacking players in free play tend to develop a more fluid type of receiving, frequently swerving as the ball is taken to switch the direction of the attack or avoid the ball's being intercepted. Receiving is one of the most crucial elements of technique and it should be stressed that it is fundamental to successful play because all that is to follow is dependent upon immediate, close control of the approaching ball.

Good receiving is epitomized by the perfectly timed interception which enables a player moving at speed to collect and move away with the ball under absolute control. Precise anticipation is required to ensure contact with the ball and different methods may be employed depending upon the angle and speed at which the ball is moving and the position of the intercepting player and her speed to the ball. When moving fairly slowly and when taking small steps it is possible to stop quickly and turn the blade of the stick to trap the ball before moving on. When the intercepting player is moving at speed or wishes to avoid a tackle the blade of the stick may point in the direction of her travel so that as the ball comes across it is deflected into her pathway enabling her to maintain her speed.

Every player can envisage the times that a ball comes towards her bobbing about and deviating from its line, and frequently when there is plenty of time to cope with the approaching ball doubts flood into the mind and by the time it arrives the player has convinced herself that she is going to miss it. Sure enough those doubts become certainties and the ball scuttles by to continue merrily on its way. Good receiving is assisted by a positive attitude.

Although the practice is not used extensively, the ball can be received in the hand. If taken in the air, it may be caught or cushioned by the hand but it must drop vertically from the point of contact. On the ground the ball is usually caught in the hand by having the fingers spread close to the ground so that the ball can be clasped momentarily to prevent any rebound. The hand can be placed with the wrist nearest to the ground so that the fingers close over the top of the ball, but there is more chance of the ball bouncing away and the receiver has to crouch near the ground, thereby restricting any movements she might need to make should the ball deviate from its line of approach. A player may stop the ball with her hand and play it herself, but most frequently this is a combined operation between two players. The receiver must stop the ball without her body being in the way of the striker. As this is most frequently used at corners it can be seen that having the ball hit from the left enables the receiver to keep her body out of the way. It is possible to do this from the right if the receiver has her back to the hitter with her fingers touching the ground and having stopped the ball she sways back to allow the striker a clear view of it. The ball must be stopped dead and a great deal of practice is required to perfect this technique.

How the ball is received will depend largely upon the subsequent actions which need to follow the collection of the ball. It is obviously easier to face the incoming ball, but this is rarely possible or indeed advisable in hockey for two reasons. Firstly, a player hardly ever wishes to send the ball straight back to its original starting point and so the feet should be organized towards the preparation for the next action as it is received and, secondly, a player will always try to collect a ball facing the goal she is attacking to avoid the possibility of obstruction. Bearing those points in mind we will assume that the player is always making the effort to face her attacking goal, wherever the ball is coming from, and we will note how the technique changes according to the direction from which the ball approaches.

The following points should apply each time the ball is received:
(a) feet pointing towards the attacking goal or at least having the intention of moving in that direction;
(b) feet already moving, therefore ready to make a large or fine adjustment very quickly;
(c) right hand placed lower than usual down the handle for greater control;
(d) blade of the stick facing the incoming ball;
(e) tension of grip released on contact.

To take a ball approaching from the right of the body the shoulders have to twist and the left arm reach away from the body to bring the full face of the stick to the ball. When the ball is coming in more from behind the receiver the excessive body twist can be eliminated by reversing the stick to trap the ball before resuming the normal playing position. The orthodox method used in this situation causes the ball to be collected behind the feet which is undesirable. Whenever receiving a ball coming in from behind it is essential that the player moves laterally to one side or the other so that she is not directly in line with the ball. It is then possible to bring the ball forward quickly to the front of the body instead of having it stuck behind the heels. For a ball approaching from the left the receiver will need either to let the ball cross in front of the body or move the feet inside the ball. A ball travelling straight towards a player should be taken well in front of the feet providing space for manoeuvre. Little readjustment should be needed when a pass is sent to a player as it should be accurate, but obviously not all passes are perfect. A sudden acceleration will frequently be required to enable a player to position most appropriately for receiving a particular pass and for a bad pass or an interception the reach may need to be extended by temporarily removing the right hand from the stick. There are two occasions when reversing the stick is of great advantage: for the ball travelling from right to left in front of a player where the feet cannot speed up sufficiently to get behind the ball and for the ball sent to the non-stick side of an approaching player.

Planning Progressive Practices for Stickwork

Because there are several books composed entirely of practices it is intended here only to give examples of how the degree of difficulty can be developed. It is not envisaged that each stage suggested should be undertaken by all players. For accomplished players it may be wise to move from very basic practices to pressure practices to see if the technique has been retained. Such players will need to keep returning to the practice of basic techniques in their simplest form from time to time. The drive has been chosen to show how a technique can be taken through from the simplest level to the most complex. Throughout we assume that the technique does not have to be learned, merely reinforced.

1. One ball to each player. Drive into a space; chase; collect; repeat.
   Coaching points: look for the next space before reaching the ball.

Approach the ball ready to drive in the chosen direction. Keep the ball moving as you collect and prepare to drive. Short, quick backlift . . . feet continually adjusting . . . head over the ball at impact. Vary the distance of the hit. Exaggerate the follow-through to smooth out the stroke, and have the weight of the body travelling through the drive.

2. Three players and one ball. Concentrated practice in driving to the right and to the left with the players positioned in a triangle. The ball must be sent directly to each player.
   Coaching points: the receiver has to move to meet the ball, adjusting her feet ready for the next pass which will of course be in a different direction. Actual possession of the ball should be for as short a time as possible. Triangular formation should be retained.

3. Two players and one ball. Passing to a moving player so that ball and stick meet each other at exactly the right moment.
   Coaching points: look to see where the receiver is asking for the ball. Judge pace and direction. Adjust speed of swing to allow for this. Reposition immediately to become the receiver. Note well that the receiver should neither need to hesitate in her running nor have to chase the ball. The recipient can vary where she asks for the ball by presenting the blade of her stick to the sender, and she can vary the speed at which she begins her movement for the ball.

4. Two players each with five balls positioned side by side and about $5\frac{1}{2}$ yd. (5·03 m.) from a restraining line. Driving for distance at speed. The first ball to be driven on the run before crossing the line and the distance it travels noted. Each player quickly returns to the start to repeat the activity and this continues until all the balls have been used. Award three points to the player whose ball travelled the longest distance and two points to the player who finished first.

5. Four players and one ball. Specific practice for hard drives hit square to the left and right. Player A feeds player B who dribbles 5 yd. (4·57 m.) and passes right to C who collects and feeds the ball to D. All players turn to face the opposite direction and the practice is repeated. A and B, C and D can change roles and the practice can be turned round to make the hard drive to the left instead of the right.

6. Three attackers spread across the field (not in a straight line) with a defender approaching the central player and the ball in possession of one of the outer attackers. The defender approaches as the central player receives a pass following which she must pass before the defender can interfere and both outer attackers must accelerate forwards asking for the ball. The central player can select which one to use. The ball must be played on to the stick of the accelerating player. The practice is resumed by turning to play in the opposite direction, moving each player on one place after several turns. Pressure can be lessened or increased by varying the distance the defender has to cover the forward centrally placed.

7. When receiving at a corner the source of the ball and the target are known and some preliminary preparations can be made. From whichever side the corner is taken the receiver should have her feet pointing towards the goal and not the hitter. Then if the ball is hit accurately precious time will not be wasted while the feet are moved to shoot. From the right the ball must be taken by the left foot for an immediate shot to be possible. From the left the ball must be allowed to travel across the body before shooting. This can be practised until the player shooting does not even need to look up and check on the angle of her shot. She should be able to keep her head down throughout the reception and shot. Pressure can be increased by introducing a third player to rush the receiving forward.

8. Pressure practice. Two players, each with a ball, facing each other approximately 15–20 yd. (13·71–18·28 m.) apart. Rule: the ball must be controlled before being driven. Both players start together and the aim is that each player intends that the other shall have to cope with two balls simultaneously.

Stealing

Possession can be gained from the bully, from intercepting (already described) or by dispossessing the opponent directly by tackling her. The last is one of the more difficult facets of the game to practise because it cannot be done alone. Essentially there is a need to learn the timing of the tackle. Even when a partner is provided for the practice she can either try to help too much by making it easy or she can ruin it by making the manoeuvre too difficult too soon.

That specialist activity, the bully, where two players without interference from others are given an equal chance of winning the ball should not deteriorate into a tackle. The skill of successful bullying lies in stealing the ball before the opponent can touch it. Only when the two players involved arrive with their sticks on the ball at the same time should tackling become necessary. Various ploys are tried in order to gain an advantage at the bully and it has to be admitted that those who have a number of tricks up their sleeves are the successful ones. When meeting such an expert it is wise to be alert and make the first two movements with the stick slowly and fairly high above the ball but make the last touch very quick and close to the ball. Do not be lulled into a sense of false security. Beware the strong player who may knock away your stick vigorously on the third tap to delay your movement to the ball, or the player who hooks her stick on the third movement to block your access to the ball. Though this is a foul it may be done too quickly to be noticed by the most astute umpire. Within the framework of the rules the following methods may be tried at the bully: pulling the ball to the left to pass it or to travel with it; reversing the stick to send the ball back to the supporting defender; pushing the ball between the opponent's stick and right foot; levering the ball over the opponent's stick when simultaneous contact is made. Pushing the ball between the opponent's feet can be rather negative as it frequently leads to obstruction by that opponent, which will stop the flow of an attack even if the free hit is awarded.

Choose the method you intend to use before taking up your stance and make sure the ball is not sitting in a hole. Place it on the highest bit of ground available so that you can make maximum contact with the surface of the ball. For the pull to the left have the feet a little further from the ball, still allowing the arms to be flexed for the snatching action to follow. When the ball is pulled away the left foot can step aside allowing an immediate push pass to be made ahead of the left inner. When pushing to the right, stand closer to the ball so that stronger leverage is possible. In addition it may help if the right hand is placed further down the stick. Knowing which method you intend to use, on the third movement of the bully the stick head must be manipulated to meet the ball correctly. This has to be done very quickly, especially if it is to be reversed for a backward pass. Look out for subtle innovations. Be alert, quick and on your toes ready to move. If you win the bully, remember to be quick off the mark with either a pass or a rapid dribble away from the area.

The playing position largely dictates the types of tackle that will be used most frequently. A fullback or sweeper usually meets an opponent coming straight towards her with the ball. She is able to choose her ground, decide whether to hold her position or advance to meet her opponent. This decision is affected by the related positions of her team-mates and the proximity of the circle edge and the goal. She may, by her positioning, force her opponent to try to pass her on one side rather than the other, thereby preventing her from using her preferred method of dodging. The defender will be on the alert to sense any momentary loss of control on the part of the attacker and time her tackle accordingly. A resilient stance will allow the defender to pounce quickly and reposition in the event of a missed tackle. Firmness in the tackle is essential if the ball is to be won. If a player is beaten or the ball is placed behind her for an opponent to run on to she will have to turn to make a chasing tackle from behind the retreating opponent. This also applies to forwards who run back to harass their opponents. Such tackles usually have to be made while both players are running at speed. Because of the tactical commitments the chasing player is not always free to decide on the side from which she will make the tackle. Wing halves, for example, when chasing their opposing wings will need to tackle from the goal side. This means the left half must become highly skilled at the more difficult tackle from the non-stick side while the right half has an easier task. Slow positioning or a speedy opponent may cause the initiation of the tackle with only the left hand on the stick to extend the reach. Such a measure may enable contact to be made, but continued movement of the feet will enable the tackler to place her second hand on the stick and assume greater strength and control. Being able to run at speed and yet take small steps is an asset. Those players who take long, lunging, despairing strides will find themselves stranded if they miss the ball at the first attempt. The aim in tackling should always be to gain possession and not merely to spoil the progress of the opponent.

In all tackling the eye should be on the ball and on the feet of the

opponent to anticipate any change of pace or direction which might
be made. The stick should be scraping the ground as the player
approaches the ball.

The straight tackle requires the player tackling to move in towards the stick side of her opponent and, in order to time the tackle
correctly, she must be prepared to sway from one foot to the other
very rapidly. This may even cause the attacker to lose control by
distracting her attention. She may also vary the pace of her approach
provided she is taking small steps to maintain her balance and
facilitate immediate acceleration in any direction. The defender
must not commit herself so fully to the tackle that she cannot keep
control of the ball if successful, or turn to tackle again if beaten.
When the approaching forward has good control then pretending
to tackle can benefit the defender. Swaying her hips can cause the
forward to respond to what she assumes to be a committed movement by the defender. Because the latter has retained her balance
and anticipated the response she can move quickly to tackle
the opponent unexpectedly. Normally in a straight tackle the hands
will be apart and the stick vertical as the defender moves in with
her weight behind the stick. Sometimes a jab may precede the
two-handed tackle if the ball runs loose for a moment. A well-
timed backward step may provide additional space and time for
the defender to make an effective tackle. Such a move may cause
the attacker to change her mind. Causing the attacker to be in-
decisive is the first stage of making a successful tackle. In this
particular one-versus-one encounter the player who first notices
the change of weight from one foot to the other and adapts her
movement accordingly is likely to win the ball.

Stick-side tackles from behind should be easy to master provided
that the tackling player leaves sufficient space between herself and
her opponent. As the stick is swung close to the ground the blade
should be facing the goal into which the tackling player is shooting.
When the stick makes contact with the ball the feet should continue
their running until the player is facing her opponent. This enables
her to put all her weight behind her stick when the final stages of
the tackle are made. If she cannot gain so much ground, the tackling
player can remove her right hand from her stick to give herself
extra reach as she sweeps the stick in an arc parallel to the ground to
contact the ball, either to knock it gently to the side or to trap it

against her opponent's stick until she has time to place herself behind the ball and complete the tackle.

Tackling from the non-stick side of a player presents more problems since the tackle has to be made across the body of the player in possession. Numerous methods have been devised which enable contact to be made with the ball without causing bodily contact with the player in possession or obstruction of her progress. Six useful tackles are described here.

(a) The circular tackle: the tackling player keeps two hands on her stick, runs ahead of her opponent, turns to face her and draws the ball away as she continues to run round to the stick side of the opponent. To do this effectively she needs to be faster than her opponent.

(b) The jab tackle: the tackling player keeps only the left or the right hand on her stick, the blade of which faces upwards. The stick is jabbed across in front of the player in possession to knock the ball away from her stick. The tackling player must either follow her jabbing action by running round and ahead of her opponent, keeping a good distance between the two of them, to collect the ball or she must rapidly withdraw her stick from the ball, allowing the opponent to run on, and then retrieve it. The method of completing the tackle selected will depend on the forward speed of the opponent to be robbed.

(c) The reverse stick tap tackle: the player about to tackle has the left hand at the top of the stick which has its toe facing the ground. She reaches across the opponent and taps the ball away to the far side. The ball is collected after the opponent has run on. The advantage of this technique is that it allows the ball to be played earlier and gives the opponent less warning.

(d) The reverse stick check is very similar to the above except that the ball is stopped dead rather than being knocked away. The grip of the tackling player needs to be particularly firm as her stick may need to withstand the pressure of the opponent's stick on the ball momentarily, before removing her stick quickly from the pathway of the running opponent.

(e) The reverse stick pull with one hand: instead of simply checking the ball possession is gained sooner by the ball being pulled diagonally backwards towards the tackling player. In the three previous tackles described the tackle can be initiated from behind but in all cases the right shoulder has to be pulled back away from the opponent to avoid obstruction. In this tackle the tackling player needs to be at least level with her opponent as she turns towards her. The ball can then be drawn away towards the tackling player who is already facing her attacking goal and ready to move off with the ball.

(f) The reverse stick pull with two hands is very similar to the previous tackle but the second hand remains on the stick to add more power to the action of drawing the ball away. The disadvantage of this is that the tackler needs to get slightly ahead of the opponent before initiating the tackle.

Practices for Tackling

1. The straight tackle. Two players and one ball. At a reasonable speed the player in possession takes the ball towards a goal area and the defender approaches trying to remove the ball to prevent the attacker from scoring.

   Coaching points: defender watches feet of attacker and the ball simultaneously with both hands on her stick and her stick on the ground. The blade of her stick should be facing the ball—balanced and mobile. The defender has got to have a realistic situation with the attacker being allowed to try and pass her in a variety of ways to keep her guessing as to what is going to happen and when. The practice she needs is of timing and judgement.

2a. Chasing tackles from the non-stick side. One player with a ball sends the ball ahead. Keeping the ball on the right, chase it, go beyond it and then turn in to face it before touching it with the stick. Return to line of running and repeat. Aim to leave as short a time as possible between sending the ball away and touching it again.

   Coaching points: begin the turn of the shoulders before getting level with the ball. Make sure the step which leads into the turn is on the right foot which should be ahead of the ball and across its line of travel. Pivot around the right foot to swing the hips through, following the lead given by the left shoulder.

2b. Three players with one ball. Player A sends the ball ahead and runs after it. Player B starts one stride ahead of A and chases the ball too. Player C positions to receive a pass from B in the event of her getting the ball first. The points mentioned in the previous practice apply. In addition player B, the tackling player, has to adjust her distance from player A to prevent body contact as each is chasing the ball.

Additional coaching points: put the stick to the ball as early as possible and wrap it round the ball as the feet and body pivot. Move the ball out of line of the stick of the incoming player. In order to steal time a tackling player who is unable to get ahead of her opponent can use the jab before completing the tackle.

3. The practices are made more difficult by the attacker starting with the ball in her close possession and having the freedom to swerve either way or the freedom to pass. The tackling player then needs to assess whether the player in possession intends to continue or to pass in order to judge the timing of her tackle. At this point the various forms of reverse stick tackle can be practised.

4a. Chasing tackles from the stick side. In the first practice the same procedure can be adopted as for tackles from the non-stick side.

Coaching points: chase with the ball on the left. Put the stick on to the ball and ahead of it as early as possible. Keep the feet running rapidly to get the weight behind the stick with the body facing the attacking goal.

4b. Three players and one ball. Player A sets off with the ball and two strides later player B chases on the stick side, completes the tackle and passes to player C. It is possible to do this practice with only two players so that the tackler must accelerate away from her opponent who immediately turns to give chase and tackles back. This can continue as long as the stamina of the two players lasts. On occasions it may not be possible to reach the ball with two hands on the stick. In this instance the left hand lunge initiates the tackle.

Coaching points: keep two hands on the stick for as long as possible. Keep a good distance away from the body of the attacker to avoid the possibility of playing her stick instead of the ball.

Evasion

There will be many occasions during a game when a player will need to evade being tackled or meet other players and take the ball past them. For this skill to develop, close ball control is required, coupled with the ability to change pace and direction rapidly. Ideally, then, the essentials for evading should be introduced in the early stage of learning to travel with the ball. Swerving, checking, accelerating and sidestepping can be practised alone with or without the presence of obstacles. However, inanimate objects do not respond and although it might be easy to learn to dribble around stationary objects, true evasion can only occur when another player is involved. A battle of wits can develop which is just as real as the techniques which are exercised.

A successful dodge requires less space and the attacker has possession of the ball immediately after passing her opponent. The secret for success lies not only in the close control, which is essential, but in the production of acceleration at exactly the right moment. For this acceleration to be available an opponent should never be approached at maximum speed. There should always be something left in reserve. The dodge must not be advertised and the attacker should get as close to the defender as possible before initiating the movement. When taking the ball to the left a preliminary movement to the right may throw the opponent on to the wrong foot and so allow the dodge to be completed. If the defender is not tempted to accept the bait the initial movement to the right can be continued and a successful dodge accomplished. A feint with stick or body may draw the defender into committing herself, so providing a route to get past her.

If players experience difficulty, it may be necessary to isolate a type of dodge and practise this separately. Here are a few recognized examples, but remember that successful evasion may involve a combination of these actions:

Left dodge: the left foot steps square to the left providing room for the ball to be pulled across after it, before accelerating forwards past the defender. If the defender anticipates and reaches out to tackle, the ball can be slipped between her stick and right foot instead of being taken all the way round on the outside.

Nutcracker: by forcing defender to move sideways, the ball can be sent between her feet and retrieved on the far side. Contact with the ball should be lost for the shortest possible time.

Right dodge: as above, but the ball is played to the non-stick side of the player.

Scoop dodge: the ball can be lifted slightly over the top of the stick of an opponent. This is difficult to do without advertising the intention.

Reverse stick dodge: the same as the pull to the left but in reverse. This time the right foot leads the way with a sidestep and with the stick reversed the ball is dragged to the right and then taken through on the non-stick side of the defender.

Stop-Go: a change of pace may provide the opportunity to accelerate past a defender who has been caught unawares by the sudden change of speed.

A defender may also use a dodge to make more space for her clearance, and every player has at times to avoid being tackled while waiting for an opportune moment to pass the ball.

Practices for evading

1. Each player has a ball. Keeping the ball on the stick, swerve, check, change direction and change pace in a confined space— for example, the 25 yd. area or the goal circle.

   Coaching points: be constantly aware of others to be avoided. Feel the pressure of the ball on the stick all the time. Emphasize sudden sharp moments of acceleration without losing control. Have the stick vertical and kept well away from the body.

2. As above, but three players out of the twenty or so to have no ball at all. Those without a ball aim to acquire one without breaking any hockey rules. This adds extra pressure because any player in possession has to head for spaces and at the same time be aware of several rapidly changing opponents appearing out of the blue.

3. Two versus one—the two starting in possession of the ball. The defender chooses to mark one of the two players. The marked player may choose to dodge or pass but the free forward may not travel with the ball and must receive and pass immediately. Their aim is to get past the defender and score. So some target must be provided for this.

   Coaching points: watch the feet of the defender to see where her

weight is committed. Keep the ball close to the stick. Be ready
to accelerate into and out of the dodge. Be aware of whether the
defender is trying to cut off the pass too. Judge the distance from
the defender before dodging or passing, aiming to find the last
possible effective moment.

4. Practice to enforce collection and control of the ball immediately
following a dodge. One player with a ball starts about 11yd.(10m.)
away from two defenders who are positioned one behind the
other, as in covering, and some 7½ yd. (7 m.) apart. The second
defender may not approach the attacker until the ball has passed
the first defender. The attacker aims to have sufficient control of
the ball following the first dodge to enable her to evade the second
defender. A lateral restriction of 5 yd. (4·57 m.) can be applied to
make it even more difficult. The nature of the second dodge is
dependent upon where and how the first dodge is completed.

Goalkeeping

The unique position of the goalkeeper necessitates an additional
set of techniques using the legs and feet in ways similar in principle
to those described using a stick. She has to receive the ball either
by stopping or redirecting it; to send the ball away as a pass; to
dispossess an opponent by tackling. A highly skilled goalkeeper
will be seen to stop a straight shot by flexing the knees and ankles to
cushion the impact of the ball and then, using either feet or stick,
move with the ball to secure a better angle for her clearance. This
manoeuvre is only possible if she is well balanced with the weight
on the balls of the feet and the shoulders forward. Should the ball
rebound it may be drawn back with the stick nearer to the feet
before being dispatched, leaving very few chances for any poaching
forward to snap up.

The goalkeeper frequently finds herself in a quick-reflex situation
where she does well to get her foot to the ball and prevent a goal
from being scored. In such cases the ball can fly off the foot and
back into play. By placing her foot firmly at the appropriate angle to
the ball she may be able to deflect it constructively.

Just as the blade of the stick can be exploited to send the ball in
different ways so can the kicking foot. For greater accuracy and to
offer the best chance of making a flat kick the instep (or more

precisely, the base of the big toe) is used in a sweeping action to finish with the weight on that kicking foot. When a shot is coming in flat and fast a stab kick can be used. This has no follow-through because the foot is used to dig into the ground immediately in line with the ball presenting a wall to reverse its direction. In fact the original pace of the ball is being used in the clearance rather than the strength of the goalkeeper.

One advanced technique used by very experienced goalkeepers is that of kicking across the line of the ball using the outer border of the foot, following through with a fairly high knee-lift. This causes the ball to spin off in a direction not expected by the incoming opposing forwards. Kicking on the volley or half-volley can be used to give greater power to the clearance. Usually this kick is seen when the goalkeeper has had to hand-stop a lifted ball which is then dropped vertically either on to the top of the front part of the foot or on to the ground to be struck by the same part of the foot just as the ball begins to rise. For balance and ball control the knee of the kicking leg needs to be lifted high and turned inwards. Since use of the hand has arisen it might be wise to consider how a goalkeeper can turn this necessary action to advantage. She is not penalized if the ball does not drop vertically, though she cannot propel it forwards. This gives her some scope for arranging deliberately where the ball shall drop. Though she cannot place the ball the goalkeeper can determine whether her hand is close or far away from her body when it makes contact with the ball; whether her body has turned before the contact is made; whether she catches and drops or uses the palm of the hand as a rebound surface.

The goalkeeper has to be particularly agile when moving out to meet a lone forward in possession. Though she has to cover the ground quickly, she must arrive close to that forward sufficiently balanced to be in a good position for tackling. As she gets closer to the opponent so her strides should shorten until she is ready to pause, poised with pads together, ready to move into a tackle with either foot. A firm thrust, getting the instep against the ball, is the most effective way of robbing the opponent.

Goalkeeping is a highly individual task in which each player develops her own idiosyncrasies. The type of kicker and leg-pad preferred by her may influence the adaptations she makes to the basic techniques. The solid hoof-type of kicker while giving good protection to the foot tends to be clumsy and to impair accuracy of kicking. Canvas kickers seem to be preferred for their lightness and their ability to mould to the foot. To increase their powers of protection additional material can be inserted to meet the special requirements of the individual. The greatest variations in style seem to stem from the part of the foot preferred for kicking by a goal-keeper. Her preferences will lead her to adapt techniques for her own use.

The lifting of kicks is not to be encouraged because of the proximity of other players unless great control can be exercised. Generally the goalkeeper will be seeking to direct the ball through a gap in the crowded circle or on to the stick of a free colleague who might have more time and a better opening for clearing.

An Individual Approach to Skill

Top-class players may well refine the basic techniques to suit their own requirements. Some may be idiosyncratic, others may be ostentatious, but many are clever personal adaptations which often prove particularly effective. Selecting examples is difficult because such refinements are so subtle that an observer needs to be close to discern them. They would not necessarily be obvious to a spectator and therefore we have been forced into choosing examples which were encountered through playing with the people concerned.

For example, Denise Parry would bemuse defenders by the use of her stick in the left hand only. The ball would seem to be out of reach and the defender, sensing this, would move in to intercept only to find that Denise had flashed out her stick like a snake's tongue to steer the ball away from the defender's stick. Then she would slide past with the ball under absolute control. Left wings on executing a feint to the left round the opposing halfback usually have to move away a few steps before being able to centre the ball. Not so Melvyn (Hickey) Pignon. She would swerve much further with her body so that it zoomed ahead of the ball and at the comple-tion of the dodge a quick lift of the stick would send the ball streaking across the field to the delight of the waiting forwards. Backs, being approached by a forward who has control of the ball, have been known to hold the stick vertically and move it rapidly

left and right in front of their feet. Many forwards have been mes-
merized by this and found the defender calmly removing the ball
from them.

All these players devised the technical adaptations to increase
their own effectiveness in their own particular playing circumstances.
Ultimately each player must be responsible for doing this for
herself. She must also continue to increase the range of her technical
skills. In this way she will be able to meet the demands made on her
and counter the advance knowledge that some teams may have of
her play. There is a temptation, having reached top levels of play,
for players to reject the need to practise stickwork regularly. It is at
this point in a player's career that she should seek to be absolute
master of ball and stick and be able to use her skills faster and
more precisely than anyone else. To be outwitted is not to be
disgraced, but to be beaten by superior skill hurts. It should
stimulate a player to work hard to eliminate any deficiencies which
have been identified. The basic techniques must be practised under
pressure in order to retain their sharpness and at the same time help
to keep the player fit enough to be in the right place at the right
time to use these skills to best advantage. A high level of skill gives
a player freedom. Freedom to choose what to do, when to do it and
how to do it—all of which adds to the enjoyment of the game.

3. *To Coach or Not to Coach*

HAVING CONSIDERED THE ways of ensuring sound technical expertise plus physical fitness, now is the time to look closely at the coach and the many ramifications of coaching.

An advanced coach can be described as one who can coach all levels of play, not only advanced players. Surely a large fund of knowledge and experience is of value to all. The more advanced the coach the more capable she is of assessing the needs of the group in front of her and meeting these needs. Some advance planning is necessary but adhering too strictly to detailed planning can be a mistake. It may be better to prepare a variety of ideas and methods of approach from which the most appropriate ones can be selected to suit the people and the moment. The advanced coach is one who has this range of information and imagination at her fingertips ready for immediate use.

Ideally the coach should not work in isolation. She is dependent initially on the selectors who have chosen the players she is to coach. Ultimately the selectors and the coach have the same intention— that of producing a winning team—so close liaison is necessary. In some instances the coach is a selector. Since the final group of players must have been decided on as a result of serious deliberations for a specific purpose, it seems reasonable that the coach should be in possession of this information. The assets and deficiencies of each player will be clearly known, along with the predominant characteristics of the group. Knowing this data will give the coach a definite starting point. If there are any doubts concerning the merits of certain players, a careful examination of the people involved can be made in the first coaching session so that the coach can return to the selectors to share her opinions and discuss a plan of action. Such a combined operation is likely to produce the best results.

Before an advanced coaching session, however, the coach sometimes has to make some assumptions about the attitudes and qualities of the players she is to meet. These provide a starting point for her planning and a focal point for her initial observation of the group. She should expect advanced players to have courage and persistence during play; to be sensitive to the needs of colleagues and the demands of the game; to concentrate actively throughout; to be inventive; to delight in teasing the opposition and to have a strong desire to win every encounter. An element of unselfishness is essential for effective team play, and yet the game also needs the egoist, the player who believes in herself to such an extent that she may appear to be domineering at times. She may seem to delight in showing off her skill for its own sake and yet the team benefits from this because opportunities are created that would have been missed. Such sentiments may be dangerous in excess, but in moderation can produce match winners. Teams can include players of this type, indeed they can hardly afford not to, and others must be prepared to adopt subordinate roles until they can avail themselves of the openings created by their more dominant colleagues.

If possible the coach should observe the players in more than one game as performances may vary according to circumstances. A player may be reacting to the presence of a crowd; she may be being watched by selectors and feel the need to advertise her skills or justify her selection; she may relish the personal battle with an opponent and be determined to dominate her; she may be nursing an injury and wish to contain her movements; or she may feel the need to set an example to others in her team. The coach must compare her assumptions with what is actually there. Should the coach find she has assumed too much she can then adapt her plans in order to allow for the deficiencies or she can tackle some of them during the session.

How does she decide exactly what is needed by the specific group in her charge? How much should she attempt to improve and what should she leave alone? Spotting the most important problems of the players before her is vital, particularly in a comparatively short session. In addition to the qualities mentioned earlier she needs to assess each individual player with the following criteria in mind:
(a) her skilled speed, accuracy and control with and without the ball;
(b) her work rate;

(c) her speed of reaction to changes in the state of play;

(d) her flair.

The coach also has to look at the overall picture to see:

(a) which team establishes early control of the game;

(b) how quickly and accurately spaces are seen and used;

(c) which players are particularly good and which are weak;

(d) how helpful players are to their colleagues when not in posses-
    sion;

(e) how easily the interplay between adjacent groupings on the
    same team develops;

(f) the shooting power, shooting quality and shooting rate;

(g) the speed of group reaction to a change from attacking to
    defending;

(h) the speed of response to the whistle;

(i) the variety of tactical moves used;

(j) the successful conversions at attacking corners or the develop-
    ment of counter-attacks from defending corners;

(k) the speed and success of taking or foiling free hits;

(l) the strength of support for an attack provided by the halfbacks;

(m) the depth of cover when defending;

(n) the sound positioning of players relative to the current play,
    especially at times when close marking is needed.

So the coach makes a general appraisal of the team and its style of
play and notes the abilities of the individuals who make up the
group. One quality demands special consideration and that is flair.
It is difficult to recognize flair and even harder to define it. Flair is
seen when something unexpected is created out of a situation and it
is the product of those self-motivated responses which are not
conditioned by coaching or planned moves. It expresses the individual's own way of reading the game and may be influenced by
her psychological approach to a particular match. A player with this
seemingly rare gift displays a number of qualities: subtle discrimina-
tion leading to the production of cunning strategy; skill in con-
triving practical solutions; and immediate insight which facilitates
rapid action and the willingness to take a chance.

These risk-takers may produce a supposedly inappropriate response
to meet the demands of a situation which can be tactically advan-
tageous because of its disorientating effects on the opposition. For
example, an obvious opening is available for a pass to be made and

the opposition move to cover for this. The player with the ball notices that a smaller crack in the defensive armour may appear if the defenders continue to move as they are doing. This crack although much smaller could lead to a shot at goal, whereas the obvious pass would not. She decides to hold the ball and then slip it through the narrow gap when it appears. By doing this she risks being caught in possession and the possibility of an interception. If successful, a goal may be scored.

How each player sees a situation is peculiar to her because her findings are based on her interests, experience, attitudes, temperament and ability to read the game. Returning to the example given in the previous paragraph, the risks involved may also include the hazard of inciting criticism from fellow players or of being dropped from the team. Thus, relationships between players, coach and supporters may be influential here. Occasionally, however, players do emerge who catch the imagination by their adventurous approach to the game, by their willingness to make bold judgements instead of playing safe. Frequently this has the effect of turning a dull, pedantic game into an imaginative and enterprising encounter.

Flair is not a mantle that can be flung over the shoulders when needed. A coach can open wider horizons to players, and inculcate in them a desire to 'do their own thing', but flair will not emerge unless the players possess in some large measure the qualities previously mentioned.

If it is impossible to observe the players before the first practice session, there are many ways in which a coach might decide to structure her session in order to make important, penetrating observation possible. It might seem sensible to start by watching the two teams play a match for a short time since so much information needs to be gleaned while play is in progress. There are, however, disadvantages to this plan. Because the players are not warmed up, the game may be slow to develop. If the players have come from many different teams they may be hesitant in their moves, not knowing how their close associates will react. In fact what is seen may be very different from their normal play. There may be a very uneven distribution of the ball so that it is impossible to see the expertise of each player and there are limits to how good one can be without the ball.

Perhaps the coach would be better advised to introduce some

stickwork and/or small-sided games initially. The kind of stick-work used for this purpose should be taxing. Pressure practices, such as those described in Chapter 2, are very useful. Repetitive stick-work circuits selecting specific advanced combined skills could be used or adaptations of known skills could be taught and tried. Fig. 1 gives an example of a skills circuit. During this spell the coach has ample opportunity to see individual skill, and she can set a fast pace for the session by being closely involved in the work.

By introducing small-sided games the coach creates a situation where it is easy for her to see a great deal of group play in a comparatively short time. Though she cannot judge the full accuracy of positioning and covering, she can get a fair impression of the 'urge to surge' of players and their general reading of play. If she selects her small groups as sections of the whole game (e.g. GK, RB, RH, RW, RI, CF versus LB, LH, CH, LI, LW) she can test and assist the building of sensitivity between adjacent players. She has forced players into adapting their positioning and moves to suit the opportunities and problems arising more rapidly than in the full game. That the teams are of different numbers is unimportant. The goalkeeper could be given to the smaller team after a short spell. It might even be useful for the coach to join in and make up the numbers in order to force the pace or set in motion adventurous attacking play.

Once the full game begins the coach can finish off her list of observations with more ease because she has fewer items to notice. Some coaches prefer to be in amongst the play for a short time to experience the 'feel' of it. Others prefer to look closely from each side-line and from behind the goal-line. From the sides they see the distances and angles for possible passes accurately. From behind the goal-line the view of defending play in the circle or the effectiveness of an attack on goal is very clear.

The periods of time allotted to coaching advanced players vary according to the results expected by those inviting the coach. If the organizers of the event envisage radical changes in style or standard of play, then a longer time span consisting of several short, carefully progressive sessions will be needed. Should a few particular players need help with positional play to fit into an established pattern involving other settled players, then coaching may need to be interspersed with matches.

CAMROSE LUTHERAN COLLEGE
LIBRARY

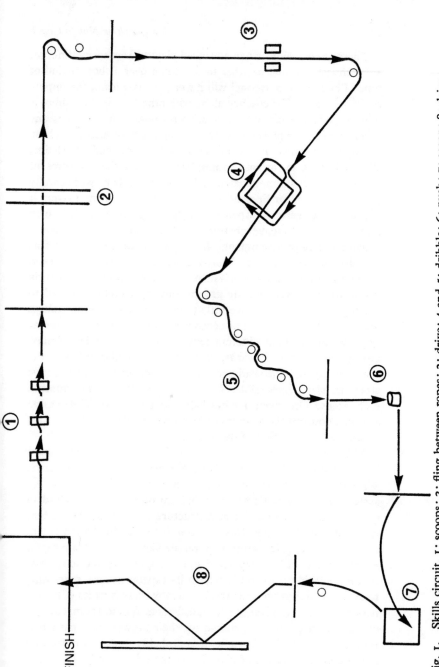

FINISH

Fig. 1. Skills circuit. 1: scoops; 2: fling between ropes; 3: drive; 4 and 5: dribble; 6: push; 7: scoop; 8: drive

There are occasions when advanced players from many different areas choose to come together for coaching over a short period of time. Though the personnel will never play as a team, the opportunity to play and be coached along with others of similar calibre is most valuable. Being able to blend with unknown players is one criterion of a good player and, since the objective of such a coaching session is the general improvement of performance and knowledge, all can benefit in an easy atmosphere without the pressures of selection or forthcoming matches. This is probably why the county players' weekend in England is so successful. For many players it acts as a pre-season sharpener to help them establish their own level of play which may be better than that of their usual colleagues.

Most coaching assignments, however, are with selected teams and although coaching at advanced level has a lot of advantages, it has one major disadvantage. The players to be coached frequently derive from several separate groups and are therefore unused to playing together. They have little time to practise together except under match conditions. The coach has to make her first consideration that of blending different temperaments and styles of play. Given three inside forwards, each of whose major assets is the snapping up of 'unconsidered trifles', co-ordinating an effective attack is nearly impossible. Who is to provide the opportunities each needs? Or, given a wing half and two backs of defensive attitude, how can the team produce a forceful attack in depth, irrespective of the location of the attack?

Any coach must be convinced that the game of hockey should use every ounce of each player's energy, expertise and intelligence. With this in mind she can look at her current assignment. No system in itself is better or worse than any other. What does lead to greatest success is to arrive at a structure which suits the current capabilities of that team. How else can that be decided upon except through severe, quick, critical appraisal? Convincing a team that it is either more, or less, capable than it thought may not be so easy. A team working consciously within its capabilities has more time to assess its opposition accurately, thereby increasing its effectiveness, which in turn gives greater satisfaction. Where a team consists of well-balanced players, chosen for their prowess in a particular position in the orthodox game, it is probably wiser to improve on their accepted patterns of play. If, on the other hand, players are chosen for their more general abilities, good blending is likely to produce less orthodox play. This may prove contrary to current fashion but may well succeed because it is based on the assets of the players. For example, with a team which has four obvious forwards and four attacking halfbacks one need not attempt to convert a halfback into a forward, but rather encourage any one of the halfbacks to add herself to the forward line as play dictates. This is dealt with in more detail in Chapter 6.

There are three possible coaching situations: namely, short term, long term and an amalgam of the two. With respect to any of these methods the coach may or may not be given a brief. Usually in selected teams there is a nucleus of players, all of whom have played together and therefore it is likely that they will retain a particular style of play which has evolved over a period of time. An assessment of the effectiveness of this combination may be given to the coach and possible needs outlined, based on previous performances. Such information may be helpful to the coach who is undertaking a short-term assignment, possibly of only one session of a few hours. For example, a team may have developed a secure defence but not been able to score goals and the coach is asked to concentrate her coaching towards producing more penetrating approaches to goal. Naturally she must retain the freedom to make her own judgements but probably she will not have had the opportunity to see the team under match conditions.

Since the encounter with the teams is to be brief and multi-purposeful, the coach's objectives must be restricted to factors which have a chance of being established in the limited time available. Also, the coach must not dismiss what the players already have as there is not time to build anything new in its place. She should simply cover for any weaknesses and enhance their strengths, at the same time leaving them with some possible developments which they can feed into their game at a later stage. To do this it is important for a coach to be able to differentiate between cause and effect, go straight to the root cause of the problem and deal with it—without removing any players from the team.

Short-term Coaching

Short-term coaching is most frequently associated with recently selected teams who are preparing for an imminent series of matches. Thus, the coach must give priority to integrating newcomers into the team, drawing upon the experience of the nucleus of players to achieve this. She aims to give enthusiasm, build confidence, stimulate thinking and a desire to play better hockey, help individuals with problems and provide some structure for the recognition and execution of tactical situations. Building confidence is a major objective in short-term coaching and can work in two ways. Newcomers must believe themselves to be an essential part of the whole team, and equally the old stagers must show that they accept newly selected players and are sensitive to their abilities and needs. All players then should learn to recognize and accept their own potential and limitations and be content to adapt their play to suit their capabilities.

Frequently players who display flair are pressured into conforming in order to be absorbed into a team, and their special skills are subdued by the rigidity of a system. Recognition of their qualities may be slow in arriving because at first sight their presence can appear to be disruptive. Once disillusionment has set in, flair is easily suffocated. A coach should nurture such players and provide opportunities within the team strategy for them to express themselves and stamp their authority on the game. Intuition is not coachable, but it must be recognized and treated with respect. Each player should define her own role in each game and be allowed the freedom to do what she feels to be right when necessary. Players who are individuals in this respect are often difficult to play with because of the demands they make on others by their speed of thought and action and by their apparent unpredictability. The coach has a part to play here in helping to integrate such players. Others need to be made aware of what may occur and their skills improved where possible to cope with the additional speed and precision required.

With single sessions the coach must make an impact on the players both as a person and through her knowledge of the game. Short-term coaching tends to perpetuate current trends in play which may in turn pass through stability to stagnation. There is not time to change the characteristic style of play of a team which after selection retains the majority of players from previous games. Faced with this situation, the coach must take what they offer, suggest adjustments in positioning and stress improved timing and accuracy with the interjection of a few clear-cut ideas to stimulate them.

If the coach intends to play safe, then her best plan might be to try to impose a rigid, preconceived style of play on this unknown, unsuspecting team, assuming them to have no outstanding individual or group preferences. If, on the other hand, she wishes to leave opportunities for their flair and enthusiasm she should take time to study the situation, allowing a freer exchange of ideas and working with the players towards producing the most effective combination.

One can deduce from this that short-term coaching has many limitations and indeed, some would query the value of a single session. Perhaps its greatest value lies in allowing the players to get together in the company of an independent arbiter who can stand on the outside and make objective, unprejudiced judgements. At the end of such a session the players should leave for home looking forward eagerly to their first match.

Long-term Coaching

Long-term coaching involves working with a team over a period of several seasons, perhaps with a specific objective in mind: for instance, preparing international teams for their four-yearly world tournament, or rebuilding a county team disrupted by a sudden influx of young and inexperienced players. Long-term coaching can lead to over-dependence on coaching and stereotyped play, but used constructively, it can provide the opportunity for:

(a) gradual building without the risk of reducing morale. For example, with a rickety defence one might have to leave everybody except the centre-half to their own devices until the centre-half can be pulled into a commanding position in the middle of the field. This may take two or more matches. Only then can the wing halves and backs see clearly their relative positions in defending in depth;

(b) the eradication of individual weaknesses is possible provided that the players are willing to co-operate and accept a likely deterioration in skill before the improvement is established. So many players think a coach can wave a magic wand over them and convert them from clowns to experts overnight. Once players are aware of their technical deficiencies, both in general terms and with respect to the specific requirements of their positional play, they will be able to devise their own practices for improving these. Do you remember seeing the left half, who has not mastered a non-stick side tackle, persistently and hopefully poking with her stick across the line of the ball whilst the rest of her tries to catch up with it?

(c) changing players from one position to another to find the best possible combination;

(d) trying specific tactical ploys in free play, using small units against varied opposition, so that the worth of the tactics can be estimated;

(e) acquiring real knowledge of each other's play as opposed to superficial knowledge. Players can develop an awareness of another player's intention by the way in which she collects the ball and moves. In this way intuitive play is possible, and players can be seen tuning in to the same wavelength and displaying uncanny co-operation, apparently without conscious communication;

(f) developing a co-operative reaction to seeing and creating spaces so that they may be used to maximum advantage. Ideally all eleven players should see the same opportunities allowed by the opposition and the same gaps in their armour, and should react both individually and collectively. The coach must be aware of the danger of unwittingly imposing her own concept of how the game should be played, for this is more likely to happen with longer contact with a team. Thus over the long term there seem to be three important ways of helping a team: to impose, to inject and to withdraw.

Squad Coaching

The term 'squad coaching' is used increasingly by various sports.

Different people make their own interpretation of the meaning of the term, but all interpretations appear to have certain factors in common: namely, a squad consists of regular coaching sessions over a period of time for selected players, the bulk of whom remain constant, with small fluctuations of membership to allow for adding new talent and discarding those not able to maintain the required standard. Differences of opinion arise with regard to the size of the selected group, the frequency of coaching sessions, the overall period of time allowed.

The squad system has much to recommend it. One of its major objectives is to ensure that all players within it are constantly aware of current tactical thinking and can experience play at high pressure, thereby maintaining the required state of fitness. The positive side-effects of regular meetings are that there is time to consolidate practical ideas and that each player in the group knows every other both as a player and as a person. Each of these tends to give confidence to those involved and should lead to greater group cohesion or 'team spirit'. Because all the players have worked together throughout coaching and practice sessions in varying combinations there should be no breakdown of this spirit, nor will there be a tentative start to matches if new players have to be co-opted. This means that selectors can feel happy about altering the personnel in the team at any stage in the season. The changes do not put the team at risk but strengthen it to cope with specific opposition or conditions. Also, because continuity of players is safeguarded to a large extent, far-reaching changes in playing formations and tactical play can be tried, tested and adopted if and where necessary. In addition it presents possibilities for building gradually to produce a greater number of high-level players. Younger or inexperienced players are exposed to the demands of this kind of play in a climate of co-operation as well as competition which helps them to produce their best play early. In this way there is a deeper layer of strong players from which to draw.

The differences of opinion which arise are closely tied to selection procedures; the willingness of players to accept such a commitment; and the problems of administration, finance and the travelling.

These factors affect the size of the group and how often coaching sessions are held. Some of the drawbacks which have been known to accumulate as a result of this system are the

C

creation of a group which is so élitist that it is cut off from the rest of the playing population, particularly if new talent is not included or fading ability discarded. Also, if the inflow and outflow of players is too great the advantages of continuity are lost and the confidence of the group can be undermined. If coaching sessions are held too frequently players become stale, find the commitment too demanding, lose interest and drop out of the game at an earlier stage than might normally be expected. Used with discretion the squad system can produce good results. If it is to be introduced it should be as a result of careful thought as a means of fulfilling certain specific needs, not because it is fashionable.

Coaching of Tactical Play

Coaching of tactical play is the hardest job for any coach. In fact it is debatable whether it is possible to do such a thing. So much depends upon what the individual perceives; what her previous knowledge and imagination enable her, consciously or otherwise, to make of the picture; the speed and appropriateness of selection from a variety of possible responses; the ability to execute the chosen solution with deadly accuracy. This sounds rather a tall order until one remembers that people are doing just this to a greater or lesser degree in a variety of contexts other than hockey every day. So should a coach interfere? Can she offer anything positive? Will any suggestions made serve only to confuse and stunt the development of an individual's natural abilities? 'Yes and No' are the answers to these questions in our opinion. This is not a classic case of sitting on the fence, it is merely an honest admission that people are different and therefore develop in diverse ways. A coach realizes that some players should be left alone to develop in their own way until they ask for or plainly need advice, whilst others need positive suggestions early on in order to set their thoughts ticking over. Very occasionally the coach may meet a disruptive player or one who presents a blank wall of resistance to her suggestions. Dealing with this is an entirely individual matter. Often the passage of time or the attitude of other players involved in the coaching session may solve the problem for the coach. A little common sense and courage go a long way in this situation.

Let us first consider perception and how to enhance this attribute. There are certain methods the coach can employ which can never produce harmful effects but which might provide positive help. Any situation where one stands to lose nothing but might gain is worth exploiting. For instance a coach can foster an attitude towards tactical play amongst players by giving justified praise whenever one player puts an opponent at a disadvantage. It may be a perfectly timed dodge or it may be a perfectly placed pass which puts several opponents on the wrong foot and catches them out of position. Once a player learns to derive pleasure from these small successes the desire to repeat the performance is likely to grow. The same attitude can be taken a stage further by urging every player without the ball to say to herself: 'If it came to me now I could carry it a couple of yards, then pass to X, who could pass to Y, who could shoot.' Ideally this would mean that every single player on the field has a constantly changing route to goal in her own mind. The fact that each of them has a different route in mind is immaterial. At least they all have the main purpose for being on the field clearly in view. Incidentally, the concentration of all players will be firmly focused and that in itself is a step in the right direction. Eventually from playing with the same people, or simply from playing more often, a certain empathy develops. All players read the same message from the same clue.

So far no precise advice has been given but opportunity and encouragement for those who have some kind of tactical ability to use it according to their own judgement have arisen. The excitement of outwitting opponents by dint of one's own efforts and the appreciation of others who can do likewise is established as an important part of the game. Meanwhile personal and vicarious experience gradually accrues for those with a reasonable memory for movement. Once a player reaches the stage of thinking 'I have seen this before' and recalling the previous response, her reaction time is reduced so her working time is increased.

To move a stage further: a coach can encourage players to look even more closely at the events taking place by constant questioning of their own current positioning. 'Where can I place myself so that the ball can come to me in order to do this, this and this?' By trial and error a variety of adaptations to basic positioning can be evolved to ensure that nobody, not even one of her own team, lies between the player and the possible pathway of a pass. Once this constant purposeful shifting of position is established more tactical opportunities are open because more players are available for use. Probably the final stage of general awareness can be achieved by each player asking, 'Where can I wait so that I am not only of most use to my own team but at the same time cause most worry to the opposition?'

Players are becoming increasingly aware of the importance of their movements when they are without the ball, especially in the continental game where man-to-man marking predominates and where the objective is to pressure opponents before they can control the ball. A greater sense of urgency is brought to bear on both the giver and the receiver since the 'cut' frequently has to be made at speed, calling for precise timing and deadly accuracy. Close marking can enable attackers to draw their opponents away from the player with the ball, helping her to create the space she needs.

We now have the basis for reading the game. The players are aware of themselves in relation to the ball and of the relative positioning of their colleagues and the opposition. This information is vital to them if they are to make the most of every opportunity as it appears.

Unfortunately there will be players who find this difficult to grasp initially with any degree of accuracy and consistency. Often such players find it helpful if the coach moves with them for quite a spell, pointing out the changing panorama, even arresting the play from time to time to explain what is happening slowly and clearly. After employing this technique the coach would be wise to withdraw her assistance completely but watch the players concerned very closely and comment when the player's adjustment of her positioning is good. This will reinforce the player's judgement without forming it for her and should lead to increased confidence giving the incentive to persevere. If she still shows little improvement, the coach could take her out of the game, removing all responsibility for reacting from her, but giving her the chance to watch another player in the same position who reacts better to play. The coach could then begin by pointing out the effective adjustments and afterwards persuade the learning player to point them out as she sees them. If this also has little effect, the coach should leave that player alone but watch her play carefully to see if her awareness develops. She may learn surely but more slowly than others, or she may be unable to make sense of the coach's approach, or she may have reached her maximum stage of development for the moment. Whatever the reason may be, further interference by the coach is not likely to serve any useful purpose at this stage. There are players who have reached their final stage of development early on and improve no more, and there are others who never cease to learn. We would not suggest discarding the former players lightly. Rather use them with discretion, placing very few on any one team. Finally we should not forget that, like the players, a coach has to be prepared to concede the occasional failure.

Theory of Tactical Situations

We can now turn our attention to gaining knowledge. Theoretical understanding of current orthodox positioning provides a good foundation for building tactical knowledge. Knowing where your own and opposing players are likely to be at various stages in the game makes recognition of any change or lapse in positioning relatively easy. Even more important is the understanding of why players occupy a certain spot and what they intend to achieve by being there. This gives a player some insight into the expectations and plans of others.

It would be foolish to be dogmatic about the exact spot every attacking back should occupy when the ball is in her opponent's circle. This would take no account of the different speeds of individuals nor their powers of anticipation. Once backs know their responsibilities they must be at liberty to display their individuality without negating those responsibilities. What is correct for one player is unlikely to be so for another. By adjusting their placing and taking calculated risks they learn the optimum position for themselves in such a situation. The coach can provide a small prod should it be necessary. With this kind of help each individual will become more knowledgeable.

Any deviations from the normal positioning of opposing players should be carefully noted so that reasons can be found. At the moment we should rule out the possibility that the alteration is a mistake. For instance why does the right inner habitually wait a few strides inside her own half of the field at the centre bully? She could be anticipating the success from the bully of her opposing centre-forward. She may be placing herself to receive a backward pass from her own centre-forward. She may be giving herself the opportunity to be across the half-way line at speed when the bully is completed, ready to collect a short, quick, forward pass from the centre-forward. Whichever is the correct reason will emerge as the game progresses and is not nearly as important as the fact that, in querying a small change, a player has become aware in her own mind of three viable tactics for a right inner to use at a centre bully.

With many players this process happens easily and they will build up tactical experience quickly with or without the aid of a coach. Other players may not have acquired the habit of questioning what they see and will welcome help, in which case the coach can assist by deliberately setting up a similar situation repeatedly. For example, a left half may intercept a pass intended for her opposing wing to find her forward impetus is carrying her towards the near side-line. A player who has no mental picture of the game by intelligent observation may persist in trying to pass to her own wing who is closely marked. At this point the coach may stop the game and restructure the situation as it was when the interception was made. As the players repeat their movements the coach can alert the left half to the spaces and free players revealed as the scene is re-enacted. Emphasis can be gained by slowing down the replay. Although frequently used, this method has certain weaknesses and the coach must try to minimize these. It is difficult to reproduce the sequence of play accurately because of the subtle relationships between space and time, particularly if the players find it difficult to remember the original situation. However the coach can set up the situation repeatedly with changes which need to be identified by the left half so that she learns to appreciate all the tactical possibilities. In this way players can see results from the same strategy several times in fairly quick succession. Though one change in positioning gives only one result, that is better than nothing at all. Initially the process is slow but once the questioning habit is formed it will be applied in an increasing number of situations. A player developing along these lines is well on the way to increasing her knowledge. The coach must be aware constantly that there are players who cannot cope with more than three possibilities. In their case too much knowledge forcibly fed could prove to be counter-productive. It may not be considered wise to repeat free play situations too accurately for their success depends on sensing the right moment for their use and they should always be open to adaptation.

Naturally set plays lend themselves most easily to being restructured as they start from a dead ball. So these can be examined with a view to offering ideas which will help the coach to set up the situation quickly and will allow maximum benefits in the minimum time. Tactical examples can be found in Chapter 5.

In the hit-out the initiative should be with defending players providing they can retrieve the ball and take the hit quickly, but this is rarely done and so most frequently the initiative passes to the opposition who have time to position to block the hit. Assuming this to be so, the practice can commence with the players positioned where they would like to be, or where the coach wishes them to be. Once a defence against the hit is established it should be pointed out to the team in possession that the player with the ball cannot by herself make an effective pass. The responsibility now falls on fellow members of her team to free themselves and create spaces. Various methods can be demonstrated by the coach, and players can be guided in their observation. This is a rather passive approach and should only be used as a preliminary because the important moment of repositioning as soon as the ball crosses the line is missed. Therefore a game should be played which provides more opportunities than usual for practising the desired tactic. This can be done by the coach having a bucket of balls available, one of which can be rolled over the end-line as soon as play enters the 25 yd. area. The new ball immediately replaces the one in play which is retrieved by an assistant while the game continues. Now the coach can ensure the defenders get the ball to the right place quickly and this can be speeded up by arranging for the goalkeeper to fetch the ball and feed it to the defender who is standing in the place from which the hit is to be taken. If the stress is on the team opposing the hit, the players not in possession must decide whether they are blocking the hit or close marking their opponents, and then reposition quickly as soon as a hit-out seems likely. Players must keep their eyes on the ball at all times if they are not to be caught napping. Having worked in this manner for a while, it may be evident that a technical deficiency is causing the move to break down so this may need to be practised separately and then absorbed back into the tactical situation. Extra practice can be gained in the initial more static practice by dividing the players into two groups working in their respective areas of the pitch—in other words left defence versus right attack, right defence versus left attack. The two teams can then reverse their roles at the other end of the pitch. Very soon the whole team should be involved to make all the tactical possibilities available.

At a corner when practising a direct stop either with the stick or hand followed by a shot, after the techniques have been mastered attackers must be pressured by the defenders. Basically the practice requires the players of the attacking team plus six defenders. Because any member of the attacking team may be chosen as the best exponent of the art of converting corners, all should be available. Once this has been established non-essential players in the practice can be released to work on other things. To keep the practice operating over a period of time without the pace lagging, the players hitting the corners should have plenty of balls to use, and two or three groups of defenders should be positioned behind the goal-line to run out in turn. This eliminates the time wasted waiting for defenders to return behind the line if a corner breaks down, and it ensures that they will be fresh enough to come out quickly. Well, at least for a longer period of time than if the same players were used over and over again. Some might say that it is good training for the same defenders to keep running out as fast as possible but this misses the point that the object is to practise converting corners in a situation which is as realistic as possible. There are better ways of training players to improve their speed or endurance.

If the attackers feel the need to attempt tactical variations at corners, then opponents should be introduced who are unaware of the plans to be attempted. When stressing defensive positioning at corners it is useful to have two full defences available so that as one group rushes out the other can watch from behind and the coach can point out any deficiencies or advantages which might be gained from a different line of running, a change in marking or a more effective start. Thus two defences can be coached at the same time and the practice retains its quality.

To summarize, when setting up a specific tactical situation for rehearsal the following points should be considered:

(a) Is it being practised in an appropriate area of the pitch?
(b) Is the simulation as realistic as possible?
(c) Are the players not immediately required made aware of what is being attempted and then usefully employed improving their own play?
(d) Are plenty of balls available?
(e) Do the players clearly understand their roles and the aim of the practice?

Conditioned Games

Coached games are ideal for the purpose of gaining problem-solving experience without the need to win being too heavy a pressure. The coach can condition the game in order to force certain tactical situations to recur repeatedly. Supposing the coach restricts wing-halves to passing only to the opposite inner or wing. This ensures frequent cross-passing. If she then removes the centre-forward and centre-half of both teams she forces the defence of each team to cover and recover very accurately, very often. From this stratagem coach and players have the opportunity of refining their attacking as well as defending positioning, the timing of their movements and their anticipation of an interception of a cross-pass.

Conditioned play is arrived at by either adding or waiving rules or by altering the numerical structure of the game. The following examples will show the variations possible within this broad description. Because they produce an unreal situation none of the forms of conditioned play should be sustained for long periods or they will create additional problems. They are designed to consolidate technical or tactical experience for individuals and the team as a whole.

Waiving a Rule

The most usual reason for waiving a rule is to ensure the flow of the game—for example, in order to allow play to continue even when the ball crosses the side-line, or when, being intercepted by a player, it rebounds from stick to feet.

Adding a Rule

This can be done in order to impose particular technical disciplines, for instance, restricting passing to the exclusive use of the drive, or for imposing a tactical discipline like restricting players to certain areas of the pitch. The latter is frequently needed for employing a zone defence. Such rules can be applied to an individual rather than the whole team by restricting her to employing a particular technique hitherto ignored by her. Similarly she could have some decision-making taken from her by being instructed to hold the ball when received, travel with it or pass immediately. Most frequently immediate passing is introduced to open up the game at speed and this necessitates accurate reading of the game and observation of the spaces left by the opposition. The coach can insist that any player who gains undisputed possession should keep the ball and go for goal, thus forcing players to have the courage to use close stickwork, and that others should support the play. A final example: forcing the centre-halves to feed only their wings, which makes them look for wide distribution and requires them to collect the ball cleanly enough to make a long pass.

Playing with More than One Ball

By providing several different-coloured balls on the field at the same time play can be switched to different areas of the pitch at a greater speed than could be managed by the players. With the attention of the players focused on the red ball the coach calls out 'yellow'. This new ball has to be located very quickly and play continues with this new focus of attention until the coach introduces a new ball in the same manner. This tests the players' ability to reposition quickly, their concentration and their stamina.

Reducing the Number of Players

Removing certain players from the full game ensures that particular conditions are created. For instance, by taking out the centre-forwards and centre-halves of each team the gap needed for cross-passing is apparent. Thus the attacking team is presented with an obvious advantage whilst the defending team sees the need to swing more quickly from side to side yet retaining its depth of cover.

Dictating the Pace of the Game

However advanced the players may be, conditioning the game so that it is played at walking pace has some value. As soon as an individual's superiority of speed over her opponents has been removed the true test of her accuracy of moving and passing can be applied. Any badly angled passes from a wing cannot be converted into seemingly good ones by a superhuman effort on the part of the centre-forward. A player who misjudges the timing of a colleague's pass and therefore starts to move too late to collect it cannot accelerate enough in order to cover her initial mistake. Though much more refined accuracy is being demanded an increase of time in which to do this is provided. Spaces diminish less rapidly, tackling players approach more slowly and so the total pressure is reduced.

Selective Coaching

A radio communications system can assist the coach in structuring a situation as realistically as possible. Instead of having to give instructions separately to opposing groups in order to enable them to work independently with no knowledge of each other's objectives, the players to be fed information can wear earphones. These clip over the ear and are battery operated enabling a player to receive information sent by a transmitter providing the wearer is inside an aerial loop which surrounds the playing area. Trying to practise a tactical move can be frustrated by opposing players either easing up to make it work or disrupting it at an early stage because of advance information. Either way the product becomes an artificial exercise of limited value. This can be obviated to some extent by offering players more than one possibility, but even then information is available to affect decisions. With the radio system information is fed directly into the ear of the player so that its impact is immediate and the information cannot be ignored. When information is fed over a distance the players can choose to pay attention or 'switch off' and direct their attention elsewhere. So the player's attention is attracted by the radio. Its greatest value lies in the fact that it can be used selectively and will only feed information to those wearing earphones. If a forward line, therefore, is trying to develop a new attacking move, its members can be coached in secret and the opposition will respond naturally. When wishing to communicate with the whole group the voice can be used normally although quieter technique needs to be developed for the microphone. A coach who in her enthusiasm shrieks 'shoot' into the microphone is likely to stimulate an unexpected response from the recipients.

Limited Area Games

Sometimes it is more expedient to leave the full game situation in order to achieve quicker experience of certain aspects of tactical play. Frequently in the full game a high percentage of play takes place in midfield and promising attacks break down at the attacking 25 yd. line, because players are not sufficiently experienced in the more demanding aspects of play produced close to goal. Concentrated practice of this nature can be achieved by setting up the following situations.

The Half Game

Half the field only is used. A full forward line plus two or three supporting defenders play against a full defence plus two or three roving forwards. The aim of the attacking players is to score in the usual way and the aim of the defence players is to score by carrying the ball over the half-way line. Play is always started by one of the players supporting the attack either from a free position or with freedom to travel before passing. This concentrated game highlights the need for forwards to tackle back, use the ball quickly and reposition speedily and frequently. In addition to constant readjustments to their positioning defenders have to locate their roving forwards as opposed to the usual passing from the defending circle.

The Quarter Game

The playing space can be reduced further to utilize only the 25 yd.

area in the following manner. An attacking forward line is supported by two halves who act as feeders and fielders. The six defenders fulfil their usual roles but are provided with three goals on the 25 yd. line through which they may score. These are placed between the side-line and 5 yd. line on each side of the pitch with the third positioned in the centre of the 25 yd. line also 5 yd. (4·57 m.) in width. The attackers aim to score in the usual way. If the ball crosses the 25 yd. line, whether it be through one of the goals or not, one of the fielders collects the ball and immediately initiates another attack. This structure sustains the intense pressure close to goal for both teams.

Strict Application of the Rules

There is a direct relationship between the skills of the game, the tactics of the game and the rules which govern play. Rules prohibit certain manoeuvres and discipline the execution of skills to such an extent that they must be applied strictly at some time during a coaching session. It is essential to make each player aware of her misdeeds so that corrections can be effected. The higher the standard of play, the greater should be the knowledge of the rules so that the game is not punctuated by the whistle at frequent intervals.

Certain rules have greater implications than others in advanced play. In interpreting the obstruction rule the distance between the opposing players concerned and the speed of the action are vital factors. Frequently in a defending circle a covering back is hovering ready to tackle while her halfback is currently engaged in dispossessing an opposing forward. Play is advancing towards the covering back. If she refuses to drop back and the opposing forward succeeds in keeping possession the covering back will by then be too close to the play to avoid committing a third-party obstruction. The back should be taught to readjust her positioning so as to make an effective tackle without breaking the rule. Players who carry the ball very close to their feet on the right of their body are likely to be shielding the ball, thereby preventing an opponent from getting close enough to tackle. They should be made aware of this so that they can adapt when necessary.

The offside rule is one which can be incorporated in tactical planning and can be used in both a positive and a negative way. Positively, a player can operate very close to the boundaries of the rule, hovering just onside before running on to a pass after the ball has been played. This pressures defences and may cause them to retreat or withdraw some support from their attack. For the attacker this is an exciting game to play involving speedy repositioning, making deceptive false cuts for the ball and streaking off the mark at precisely the right moment. It is inexcusable that a promising attack should come to nothing because a player is caught offside, particularly if she is some distance from the focus of play. Remember though that a delayed pass can cause a player to be offside as well as a badly timed run for the ball. Players may be caught offside if they exploit this rule to maximum advantage, but it is a risk worth taking.

Negatively, defenders can capitalize on the rule by deliberately trapping players offside. This is achieved by moving forward just before the ball is played to leave only one defender between the attacker and the goal. This is risky for care must be taken that the intended victim does not anticipate the action, that she is not inside her own half or behind the player with the ball. Both teams can play the offside game and it is essential that all the ramifications of the rule are understood.

The most frustrating of all infringements is that of lifting the stick too high on a drive and this does happen even in advanced games. Corner hits, shots and free hits from inside the defending circle are frequently wasted. This is a complete waste of the energies of the team. Guilty players must be made aware of this and given positive help as suggested in the chapter on stickwork. As an interim measure it might be sensible if they adopted a grip with both hands well down the handle producing a reduced swing. If this bad habit is not eradicated the players concerned may have to avoid using the drive at all with the many consequent problems.

Rules are broken during matches, sometimes intentionally. This is a great pity since the rules are there to determine and define the boundaries of competition. The coach should foster amongst her players the desire to outwit and outplay opponents who foul deliberately. Superior skill should triumph providing that the rules are rigorously enforced by the umpires. When an illegal act ceases to be profitable it ceases to be used. Perhaps a team which has to resort to breaking the rules in order to win matches does not win at all since it is really playing a different game.

Meeting Your Match

Because during matches players have to take the responsibility for their decisions, it is important that they do this frequently in realistic practice sessions, knowing that there will be no interruption and no comment until the end of the session. Players will be making considered judgements throughout the game, evaluating the effectiveness of their play in detail. For example, were they more successful with the simple methods or the more complex? What would they reject as being unworkable for them? Could this same thing be made effective with slight adaptation and further practice? What was good as opposed to what was just acceptable? Did the end result reflect the endeavour? This is where the coach plays an important role as the recipient of all these opinions to which she can provide a boost by her agreement, give added confidence, or sow the seeds of doubt where the outcome of events was less clear-cut. In order to be able to do this, during the practice session or match the coach has retired to the side-line with her flask of strong coffee. Here is her opportunity to learn a lot about the players. Seeing them under pressure she can judge their capacity to:

(a) sustain the use of new ideas;
(b) probe the opposition perpetually with glee;
(c) read the play, effectively selecting appropriate tactics;
(d) produce spirited play even in adversity;
(e) grow in stature as the game progresses;
(f) react spontaneously to seize an opportunity or give support to a colleague in difficulties.

In addition she has to take an overall view of the play, deciding which tactical ploy she considers to have been truly effective, where praise for initiative and spontaneity is merited and whether there is real cohesion. If the team gives the impression of being in command of the game in spite of changing fortunes then the services of the coach may be needed no longer. Should this not be the case then her observations will provide her and the players with suitable material for further work. The essential part of this whole process is the coming together of players and coach to share opinions in an atmosphere of honesty. Most players at top level have constructive ideas which should be tapped. The atmosphere of sharing tends to bring out the best in a group and can trigger off a flow of other ideas, which may either be used, adapted or rejected. This is why the coach should drop in ideas occasionally and leave the players to sort out various interpretations, which must then be unique to them. For instance, the coach in practice sessions can set the scene. 'Suppose you meet a team which habitually retreats in defence.' Then she sets the tasks. 'Work out several attacking ploys to cope with this.' Such a method forces players to think beyond their current experience while they still have the advantage of an objective view from the coach. There are times, however, when no more advice should be given, allowing time for the current standard of play to meld—but not to mould! Every match the coach sees will increase her knowledge and understanding of the players.

The Role of the Coach during Matches

Each game presents opportunities for players to increase their fund of experience and employ their imagination. Over a period of time a great mass of knowledge and information is built up by each individual for spontaneous use at any time. There is no substitute for time and match play for acquiring realistic experience. Coached games can serve very useful purposes but one must admit that many players produce better hockey during match conditions— though others do not. Since match play is the whole point of the game, experience gained through it is of greater value than that acquired in any conditioned game. Can a coach play any useful part in this situation? This is a question which evokes very strong opinions. Many people who come out firmly against a coach having any contact with players before, during or after a match have a deep-rooted fear of producing a race of players who are nothing more than puppets manipulated by 'the master' on the side-line. It has been seen to happen in other games, notably American football, so the fear is justified. Would any real lover of hockey want to participate in a game controlled from without? One would doubt that very strongly but it is not beyond the bounds of possibility that a coach could become so involved that, inadvertently, she directed the play from her perch. Would any player willingly walk on to the field knowing she was not allowed to use her own knowledge, judgement and expertise? Could she possibly derive any satisfaction from being a mere extension of someone else's personality and planning? It sounds highly unlikely and yet one must recognize that it is possible for some people to be overawed by a strong personality, or even to possess an extreme sense of loyalty which can result in subservience. There are others who are only too glad to let somebody else take the responsibility, especially when failure is a distinct possibility. All this being so one can sympathize with such an opinion.

It seems to us that there is a case for a coach helping with matches so long as she has no intention of dominating and the players have no intention of being dominated. Advice given by anyone should be carefully considered, possibly tried and certainly rejected the moment it is found wanting. This the players must do for they, and only they, are finally responsible for the effectiveness of the play they produce. Supposing a coach, before a match, describes the opposition as likely to be strong, technically very sound and quick to meet the ball. This information is not a figment of her imagination but a result of trends noted over a period of time or of a recent match played by the opposing team. Once the match has begun and this partially known opposition produces inferior play, quite different from that which was expected, surely the players can recognize this and discard the advice given. In this instance the coach's prediction was quite wrong. At the very least it might have had some value in that it prepared the players for a harder match than the one that ultimately emerged. The team's tuning to a higher pitch should have made it easier for them to defeat their opponents. Where the coach and the players pool their sources of information about the opponents before a match a truer picture is likely to emerge. On the basis of this several possible tactical ploys can be discussed in detail to be used or not at the discretion of the players. The real advantage of this pre-planning lies in the fact that everybody is aware of more than one method of dealing with a situation which is likely to arise. It is equally important to note that pre-planning does not preclude reacting spontaneously during the match. It acts as a sort of nest-egg in the bank should the current account run low. So long as an atmosphere of mutual trust amongst the players prevails the pre-match planning can be an asset.

Before the match when a team is working out in practical terms ways of coping with a particularly dangerous opponent or of counteracting an expected tactical formation, the coach can be of great service to the team in two ways. She can add her suggestions to theirs for trial. The more ideas that are explored, the more likely a large number of sensible possibilities will arise from which to select. In addition, she can assist in checking the effectiveness of the team's plans, particularly if they are unknown to her in advance, by becoming an opposing player in a key position. It is very easy for a group of people bent on making a tactic effective unwittingly to structure their colleagues acting as opposition in such a way that the ploy will succeed. When the coach joins the opposition, interested only in the hockey around her, she will react quite naturally as the play dictates, thereby proving or disproving the viability of the operation in whole or in part.

Usually it should be unnecessary for the coach to see players at half-time in a match. The captain and players themselves should be able to cope efficiently. However, in certain circumstances, access to a coach at this time can be of value. Individual players may wish to pick her brains about a particular opponent who is too troublesome and who has refused to nibble at any of the bait so far offered to her. Discussing with the coach the wisdom of using a particular team strategy might help to clarify its effectiveness and give the team confidence to persist. Advice on slight alterations of timing for certain moves might be a boon. A small morale-booster might not go amiss. There is no doubt that the informed observer can have a very good total picture of events along with a certain amount of detachment. The coach may therefore have noticed some quiet but significant manoeuvre by the opposition which has escaped the notice of the players so heavily occupied on the field. For instance, the opposing defence may be shielding their goalkeeper from attacks more fiercely on her right than her left. This information could lead the players into building up attacks on their left but switching the play over to the right at the last minute in order to probe this seeming weakness.

At half-time players and captain will have much to say to each other concerning the second half of the match. If the coach happens to be present she can listen carefully following their reasoning, being ready to give her views if asked. Sometimes she may feel it necessary to offer her opinions uninvited. If she feels a team is sitting down under its difficulties or creating more problems for themselves than the combined efforts of the opposition she should say so. Such words may provide the very stimulus needed to spur the players on to greater effort on the one hand, or bring them back to reality on the other.

A formal post-mortem after a match can be a most depressing and false occasion. Nevertheless the players in their informal groupings will conduct one. In fact they will probably pick up the whole game again weeks later and still find pleasure in reminiscing. Certain incidents seem to remain forever etched in the memory. Some years ago a wing-half inadvertently hooked her stick around the ankle of her captain while waiting behind the goal-line for a corner hit to be taken. Result: one back (the captain) flat on her face; one puzzled halfback apologizing profusely; two opposing sticks unattended. Disaster was averted. Perhaps the humour of the situation disturbed the opposing team's concentration. Who knows? We were left in no doubt, however, that this was not a tactic to be repeated.

One might ask what possible place a coach can have in discussions after a match. She was not an integral part of it. Perhaps she should leave the players to find out for themselves what they have learnt. This could well be the best course of action, particularly if the match was a success. On the other hand some teams have a tendency to become too intense, seeking errors in their own play where there are none. A little level-headed comment from an arbitrator can often ease them through this stage of uncertainty. There was an occasion when a few county players from two recently opposed teams used adjacent bathrooms. The winning team had collected a score of ten goals to one against in a very taxing match. The defeated players were soothing their wounded pride in the hot water, quietly wondering what more they could have done. Meanwhile the serious discussion from the neighbouring bathroom harbouring players from the winning team floated clearly through the walls. They were solemnly isolating the possible flaw in their make-up that allowed that one goal to be scored and planning ways of improving their play. As it happened they achieved the improvement but one rather wonders how much was due to that intense parley.

When a team is involved in a series of matches following in quick succession it is important that they reassess their abilities and shortcomings as individuals and as a team in the light of performance during the match. They must count their assets and consider their defects while all is still fresh in their minds. Most players of good calibre will do this anyway but time needs to be made available for collective discussion. How and when this is done will and should vary. We believe there are times when the presence of the coach is valuable. She can serve the same purposes as at half-time. Firstly she can act as a sounding board for testing players' opinions and ideas; secondly she can offer her honest appraisal of the play; and thirdly give praise where it is due. In addition she could, where necessary, give technical advice to an individual player whose stickwork deteriorates under pressure. That player will have time before the next match to put in some hard practice, rebuilding her confidence into the bargain. This might also be a good time to be thinking of the forthcoming opposition so that all players have the opportunity to consider quite calmly possible tactics in the interim period.

In this chapter it has been suggested that a coach could be a very useful appendage to a team on many occasions. One is well aware of the dangers of too much coaching and too much direction of the players. Most coaches are aware of this and the need to allow players to use their initiative. It is important that they continue to be so. The game of hockey keeps our interest because it remains an unknown quantity. It is impossible to know all the answers or even all the questions. Once a team takes the field for a match the play will indicate the effectiveness of the combined efforts and prowess of the players. The beauty of the game lies in its unpredictability. No amount of planning can ensure success though it can increase the odds in favour of this. Collectively coach and players share the successes and failures with the selectors. Success is often interpreted as winning, whereas in reality it can be the scoring of more goals than ever before or producing better play in all respects. Proving to be worthy opponents can be a tremendous achievement; nevertheless we would expect a team to play a match trying its utmost to win.

The length and intensity of coaching depends on so many variables such as the availability and commitment of the players and coach, the distances and finances involved, the relationship between players and coach. The appropriateness of long-term coaching, short-term coaching or an amalgam of the two is bound to fluctuate according to the personalities involved. So it would be foolish to recommend any one particular kind of coaching without being in possession of all the facts. Those who have the facts must accept the responsibility for whatever decision is made. Above all it is important that objectives are clearly stated so that all those involved can have a unity of purpose.

4. *Tactical Taxing and Teasing*

IN CHAPTER 3 we touched on the coaching of tactical play. In this chapter we propose to look in greater detail at the nature of tactics, the attitudes of players towards tactical play, the development of tactical awareness linked with the role of each player, the principles upon which tactics are based and the place of the coach in assisting this growth.

The desire to see one's opposition constantly in a state of anxiety or difficulty is one of the simplest objectives of the game. For this to be achieved one's own team needs possession of the ball for a large proportion of the time. Ultimately the aim of the team will be to make the opposition play the ball within a few predetermined limits set up by the approach play and group positioning. Once this is achieved too much energy need not be expended on denying the opposition possession of the ball. That energy can be held ready for tremendous surges of powerful attack.

Tactical Thinking

What are tactics? There are many very obvious answers to this question and almost all of them are viable. Perhaps a simple definition might be the combination of personal and collective skill, plus quick, accurate, persistent observation of the opposition, with the imagination and courage to act on decisions made, together with trust in the good sense of companions. Mixing these ingredients with the intention of teasing the opponents from beginning to end of the match will supply the means of beating them. Yes, it is taxing for players, physically and mentally, but perhaps this is where the real fun and the real skill lie, especially as each player means to make it more taxing for the opposition than for herself. Thus she gives the opposition too little time and energy to tease in response. Never let them know exactly where you are. Convince them that there are more tricks up your sleeve than they can imagine and one game is not long enough for half the ideas to be used. Enjoy reacting spontaneously and positively to any unexpected play the opponents try to produce. As most people realize, meeting entirely predictable play in the opposition leads to a certain degree of boredom, which leads to diminished concentration, which in turn leads to mistakes. This seems to suggest that boring the opposition in itself might be a tactic and we suppose it could be effective. No tactics have an absolute guarantee of success but the latter seems to be more risky than most. The players employing this tactic may succumb to its effects themselves and are certainly less likely to have maximum fun during the game. Meanwhile there is the risk of giving the opposition the opportunity to settle as a unit. Recall some association football matches where exactly that appears to have happened, whether by design or accident.

In simple, general terms the most effective tactics are those which build up attacks quickly using the full width of the field. Moral one: if the goal circle can be reached in three passes or fewer, do not use more. Moral two: use the wings early and often to tax the stamina of the opposing side halves, thereby making their capability of good defensive covering suspect. Moral three: if the opposition retreats, take the play to them and force them into dealing with your attack earlier than they would prefer to do. In effect, make them change their normal style of play early on so that you can retain the main ingredients of your own style. The initial effort is worth while because sustaining pressure becomes easier as the match progresses once you have the initiative.

Eventually when players retain full awareness it is possible to reach a state where there is no need to fear the opponents' having possession of the ball because it is possible to force them to play it when and where you will. For instance, by approaching a tackle in a particular way one can force the possessor to move towards or to pass towards a colleague who is supporting closely; or a group of four players can position so that no effective pass can be made by the opponent in possession and neither can that player retain possession without avoiding two tackles in close succession. We would consider this to be taxing the opponents in every way.

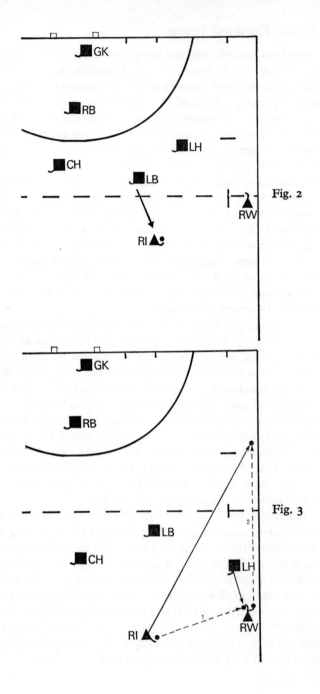

Fig. 2

Fig. 3

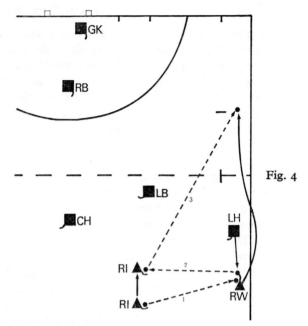

Figs. 2–4. Defending players positioning to force the opposition into predictable play

Being ready to adapt one's play is vital but to change with too little provocation can be dangerous. The times one stands on the side-line saying 'Not again' as the same trick is tried and fails a third time remain imprinted on the mind. And the other occasions, when circumstances have changed subtly, and one sees so clearly that a repetition of that previously foiled play would be most likely to succeed. For example, there is the right wing who sends a straight pass close to the side-line several times, in spite of the fact that her opposing left half is in position to deal with such a pass. It is foolish of her for, amongst other things, it discourages her from using that very pass effectively seconds later when the opposing left half has been drawn further into the field. Passing for its own sake and the interesting pattern it makes is a common trap into which many teams fall. Why not go straight for goal unless the tackling or positioning of the opponents prevents this? It is just possible that a team is following the dictates of habits formed by playing other very different opposition even though such ploys are inappropriate to the current situation.

Assuming some skill, however limited, taxing and teasing the opposition is not only possible but essential if the real purpose of the game is to be appreciated. Nobody would deny the tremendous excitement of running very fast nor the pleasurable sensation of a hard drive or clever, close, manipulative play. We maintain that any of these indications of prowess can allow a player a maximum of 50 per cent satisfaction in a game. The full appreciation can come only when that long run is part of anticipating and collecting a long pass; when the hard drive reaches its recipient having tempted opponents to move out of position and therefore shattering their neat little pattern; when the clever, close ball control has been quick enough to eliminate at least one opponent leaving the player in undisputed possession with time and space to choose the next move. This recognition of what one's actions do to the opposition is the crux of the whole matter.

There are twenty-two people vying for the same working space, the same ball and enough time to put that ball between the goalposts. As soon as one set of eleven players accepts that the other eleven intend to monopolize the situation and simultaneously decides to be dominant itself, then a good tactical climate is created. To win a match one must have time, space and the ball. The opposition will try to deny a team all of these things; therefore opponents must be the first and permanent focal point of your concentration and your wits. Individual skill, whether the range be small or large, should be sure and accurate enough to allow the mind to operate quite freely. It should have to consider techniques only in the context of 'which shall I use?' not 'how shall I do it?' A group of players capable of driving and pushing the ball and of swerving in possession, if they are prepared to work within their technical limitations, can be as effective a team as a group of players having a full range of technical skills. The number of techniques mastered by each player can be less important than the accuracy of timing, pace and direction in their execution in relation to the opposition. Difficulties arise when the opponents have equal or superior accuracy plus a wider repertoire. We should stress that we believe a good range of skill should be acquired as early as possible but not at the expense of accuracy.

Assessing an Opponent

It is important to know your own capabilities and those of others in your team but the opponents are the essential ingredient in the game. They provide the excitement so it is essential for each individual player to learn about them separately and collectively. Presuming that you know yourself pretty well you can turn your attention immediately to the opposition. Anything you may know prior to the game can be of assistance in your judgement, provided it is used sensibly. It is dangerous to count on that foreknowledge as being a fact. What is true of an opponent in one match on a specific ground in particular weather conditions with one group of companions is not necessarily true at any other time. All that is known is that certain reactions and abilities are likely to be apparent. One can plan ahead several ways of countering this opponent and make it one's business to check her current form the moment the match begins. Watch her like a hawk. Take the play to her. Test out her supposed strengths and probe for her potential weaknesses as early in the game as possible. Only then will you know her standing in relation to you and your team. Only then will you know which plans for outwitting her are needed. If it transpires that she lives up to her reputation, nobody is caught unprepared; if she does not, then she can be placed lower on the danger list, saving mental and physical energy for yourself.

The scrutiny of an opponent needs to be very exact. What is her speed relative to yours? Is she slow or quick off the mark? Is she quick to turn and give chase? Your play will be strongly affected by these answers. Assuming the worst—that is, her score is higher than yours on all counts—then your positioning will need to be adapted and adjusted many times during the game. Rarely can success be achieved in this ploy unless one's companions are also aware of the difficulties. For instance a left wing with this extremely effective opponent using her normal positioning cannot expect her favourite long run to pick up the pass close to the side-line inside the opposing 25 yd. area before making a cracking pass across the back of the circle. That wretched right half will be there to harass, spoil the play or steal the ball. There are several schemes the wing might try in order to foil the opponent. She might position very close to the opposing right half, almost in line with her (taking care not to be caught offside), ready to cut behind her towards that same long ball earlier, meeting it further in from the side-line, ready to go on with the ball across the field or pass before she can be tackled. In so doing she will have shattered the prowess of the good halfback by earning for herself the time it takes the opponent to turn, and using this time either to move out of that opponent's precinct or to send the ball out of her area. Alternatively, the wing may choose to increase the space between herself and the right half by lying closer to her own goal, tempting the half to position with less depth. If the halfback succumbs to this temptation, she leaves a lot of space behind her which can be used by the enemy. For instance the attacking left half could take over the job of the wing momentarily to receive from the left inner and distribute the ball rapidly. On the other hand the wing could move back to receive a slightly backward pass which can be lofted into that large space so that the left inner can move out, collect it and continue in the guise of the wing.

If the right half does not alter her positioning, the attacking team may decide to give the left wing shorter, straighter passes so that she can cut in front of the half and play on from there. In using this ploy the wing will have conceded some victory to the half who has virtually prevented the attacking team from using the full width and depth of the field. Each of these tactics may be effective or none of them, but at least one vital message will have been delivered to that excellent right half, namely that the attacking team is not prepared to ignore its left wing because of her. Though taxing to all concerned, the teasing will continue until the half is more taxed than the wing. The gradual wearing down of a good opponent has begun and she knows it. She can never cease to be concerned with what the players in her immediate vicinity might be doing next.

Now the need to check the opponent's skill with stick and ball arises. Is she strong in the tackle? Is she clever at avoiding your tackle? Does she need a lot of space in which to work? Is she quick and accurate in her distribution of the ball? Does she have a favourite dodge or pass? Does she vary the pace and place of her passes? Is she vulnerable on the non-stick side? If she appears to have few failings judged by these criteria, once again your positioning needs careful thought to ensure she never receives the ball and so cannot use her skill. Though this would be a cause for concern for every player, it is particularly important to a defender. Suppose a centre-half is trying to cope with such a clever opponent. She may have to back up her own attack more deeply than she prefers in order to cut off any counter-attacking passes heading for the centre of the field. Even though the centre-half is between her opponent and the ball she needs to remain fairly close to her in the central area of the field, giving herself the best chance of intercepting passes and, if that little bump in the middle of the field betrays her, allowing the ball to reach her opponent, she is in a very good position to harass her quickly and persistently. When she is in defence and therefore marking between her opponent and her own goal she must be certain to place herself far enough to the ball side of that centre-forward to allow herself the chance to make a clean interception, remembering that the centre-forward may dart towards the ball. Her close marking at this point may well mean she is more than a yard to her left-hand side of the centre-forward in order to move forward to the interception rather than have to run on a lengthy arc. She should avoid being so close to her opponent that her own movement is restricted. Any centre-half as close as that is easy prey for tackling. In fact she is making her own life difficult and has become an asset to the opposition.

The picture of an opponent is now filling out beautifully. Bearing in mind the need to know her better than she knows herself, we pass on to testing her resistance to mental pressure. This can be considered as her match-playing maturity. It does not necessarily have any correlation with her length of experience in match play or her age. Some players show maturity very quickly, some never achieve it, others lose it and then regain it. So it is always worth while to test this particular attribute early in a match. Can she be flustered by a little harassment? Can she be tempted into holding the ball and over-using close stickwork? Can she be forced into running in a particular direction repeatedly? Does she lose heart when a few attempts at constructive play have failed? Once this information can be added to that on her physical capability the filing card is complete and the player holding this card has begun to make herself worthy of being on the field. The opponent remains and is still a force to be reckoned with but she is no longer an unknown quantity. This in itself should give confidence to a player in addition to opening various possible ways of nullifying the opponent's effectiveness.

The first ten minutes or so of the match have now passed and our player must widen the horizon of her scrutiny. All the opponents in the immediate vicinity need to be watched with equal care when they are playing the ball and when they are not. Repetition of certain moves or techniques can be noted in addition to the mental attitudes expressed by the way in which the latter are executed. The final stage in knowing the opposition is reached when every single opponent has been subjected to the player's personal microscopic examination. This rigorous discipline, if applied by each player in a team, leads to more freedom. The game itself will almost always produce the unknown and the unexpected in patches so the wise team will give itself maximum opportunity to react to these situations by knowing as much as possible beforehand.

Because the play is rapidly moving, some means of recognition of opponents must be sought. Watching the ball and playing the ball casts the eyes downwards so facial recognition is not always possible. Socks and skirts or shorts will be the same on each opponent. The boots and their lacing, the feet and the legs will differ. There is real advantage to be gained from noting such simple signs. For instance the moment a left inner in possession of the ball sees the opposing centre-half's boots approaching her for a tackle a smile of satisfaction should light up her face. She knows her own centre-forward is likely to be free for an easy pass and she knows to some extent how the other defenders are likely to cover this indiscretion on the part of the opposing centre-half. This momentary weakness by the opposition can be exploited to the full. Centre-halfbacks the world over send up silent votes of thanks to opposing inners who, in such a situation, pound the ball out to a wing.

A team gaining most tactical advantage consists of people each of whom is constantly and clearly aware of a minimum of nine players. Some will be her own players, some will be part of the opposition but all are extremely relevant to the current situation. The higher the level of the game and the faster it moves the more this numerical awareness is needed. If the position of players is known, then the spaces are known.

Informed spectators have an easy time seeing this. They have no responsibility for playing the ball or for making vital decisions. Nor do they have a share in shaping the result of the match. For the players involved the task is not easy. Nevertheless, it has to be done. It requires intense concentration, courage, speculation and skill. Information gleaned is of no value until it can be put to practical use. It is in this area of ability that the outstanding players and the outstanding teams are discerned.

Orthodox Tactics in General Play

If we accept that in the main the simplest tactics are most likely to succeed, just as the simplest mechanism breaks down infrequently, then we must accept that current orthodox play is of value. The words 'orthodox tactics' usually apply to those tactics which are most likely to succeed in most circumstances. The rules of hockey do not dictate how the eleven players in a team shall be placed or deployed so long as they begin the game within their defending half of the field and return to that half of the field for each centre bully. Though we may be on the brink of change in what is considered to be orthodox play, at the moment we still tend to present five forwards, three halfbacks, two backs and one goalkeeper, placed in receding order of width and depth from the centre-line.

The Forward Line

During play the forwards keep roughly equidistant from each other with the outside players, the wings, moving outside the side-lines of the pitch. In order to create more space through which the ball can travel the forwards do not keep in a straight line relative to each other. Some pull nearer to the opposing goal whilst others lie nearer to their own goal-line. This means there will be the usual space ahead of the most forward-lying players plus space behind them through which the ball can travel to be used by the forwards placed behind their attacking colleagues. In this way several lines of attack are presented instead of just the one. The position of the ball dictates which forwards are up the field and which are further back. Usually the players in the area of current play are further back whilst the others move up-field as far as the offside rule will allow

in order to anticipate forward passes. This general guide is relevant
only in midfield play where there is plenty of forward space available.

Forwards who move away laterally from a colleague in possession
are very useful in a team because they indicate their awareness that
creating space is a major role. By such a move they create space
either to cut into for a short pass or to allow the ally in possession
to alter her course to avoid a tackle. Undoubtedly they will have
moved an opposing defence player further away from the ball or
left themselves free for a pass. Much of the time during a match
adjacent forwards will endeavour not to be level with each other. If
each one is aware of the positioning of players nearest to the ball she
can then alter her place of readiness accordingly, taking into account
movements of the opponents too.

Sensible flexibility is most important to a line of forwards. If
all are forever bobbing hither and thither they will be most difficult
to find when needed to receive a pass. Exactly the same result will
transpire if they do not shift from one spot to another. Anticipating
play and trying to read the minds of other players is the best guide to
where and when to move. So long as the positioning is made very
decisively and for a definite purpose it is likely to be successful.
After all, forwards do start the game with the ball in their possession
so they need to manoeuvre in order to lose or eliminate the opposing
defenders.

The Defence

In order that each of the six defending players shall present one
line of defence the halfbacks lie roughly in a diagonal pattern
across the field, the backs form a less acute diagonal line and the
goalkeeper forms the apex of a mobile triangle. If lines were drawn
parallel to the goal-line through the place of each defending player,
no two of them would be found along any one line. Initially,
defending players aim to fill and mark the spaces between the
opposing attack and their own goal. It is an impossible task but,
because their positioning is staggered, defenders almost fulfil this
aim. At least they make it difficult for the opponents in possession
to gain ground by sending the ball ahead into spaces, and they
retain numerical superiority of six to five. The diagonals are decided by the place of the ball. When it is on one side of the field

1. (*top left*)   The hand-and-stick stop. Note the position of the left hand ready for a 'chopper' hit
2. (*top right*)   Preparation
3. (*bottom left*)   Point of contact of 'chopper' hit
4. (*bottom right*)   Follow-through

5. Preparation of 'fling' stroke
6. Follow-through

7. Goalkeeper positioned with heels touching front edge of line at penalty stroke
8. Front view of goalkeeper at penalty stroke. Note how the stick is held ready to use or to free either hand for a high ball

9. A push-in with the player positioned outside the line and behind the player with the ball

10. Players at the push-in have positioned so as to leave a gap for the ball to be pushed to the centre of the field

11. Players at the push-in forming a half semicircle 5 yd. (4·57 m.) from the ball with one attacking player outside the line and nearer to the attacking goal

2. The ball is not close to the goal-line so the covering back positions in the space ahead of goal to prevent an attacker from lying close to the goal without being offside to prevent a pass across the circle

3. The ball is close to the goal-line so the covering back is positioned near that line to pick up any attacker who might decide to lurk close to the goal (N.B. No attacker can be offside because all are behind the ball)

14–17. Players using maximum length of reach and clever footwork so as to avoid the opposition and get the ball into a shooting position

-20. Defending players resorting to very unusual positioning in the hope of preventing a shot at goal (*Hockey Field*)

21. Hand-stop at corner hit. Note how the 'stopper' keeps her body well away from the ball so that she will not obstruct the hitter (*Hockey Field*)

22. Defending players off to a fast start at a corner, so as to reach the attacking opponents as quickly as the ball (*Hockey Field*)

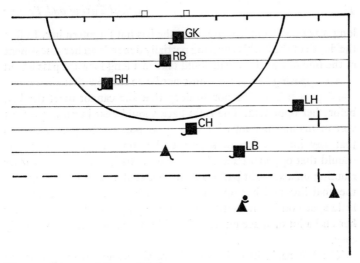

Fig. 5. Staggered lines of defence

the defenders on that side will be close to the play whilst the others will fall back and inwards toward the centre of the field. This allows the latter to cover for mistakes by their colleagues and to leave their own working space ahead of themselves. In fact, defenders aim to move forward to an interception or a tackle rather than across the line of the ball. It is useful for a defence player to assess where any ball to her personal opponent could travel and then position herself two strides further back than this so that she has safely allowed for some error in her judgement and also given herself the opportunity to be moving at speed as she goes forward to a clean interception.

Once an attack is progressing and space is at a premium most of the defenders need to mark an opponent's stick, leaving a goal-keeper and one back to mark the goalmouth and the space immedi-ately in front of it. Opinions differ even within orthodox play as to the exact positioning of the covering back, especially when the attack is mounted by the opposing right wing close to her own side-line when she has defeated the left half. Some prefer the covering back to meet the right wing in possession on the edge of the circle; others prefer to allow her the chance of a very restricted shot from the circle edge and deny her the opportunity to pass.

The covering back has to reconcile two jobs. Though she is a

D

long way away from her opponent she has not forgotten her. In fact the depth of the back's covering partially depends on her assessment of the line of travel the ball could take in a long forward pass ahead of her opposing inner. She must not be so shallow that such a ball could pass behind her nor so deep that she cannot meet the ball before her opponent. The right back should bear in mind the best way of making her own job as easy as possible by positioning so that any interception of a pass to her opponent, or any tackle should that opponent actually receive the ball, can be made by her running on a straight pathway with her stick between the centre of the goal-line and her opponent's stick. This virtually leaves very little space on her non-stick side where play would be difficult for her and a lot of space on her stick side where working is relatively easy.

The left back, in order to achieve the same advantage, has to approach her opponent along a pathway parallel to the side-line and at right angles to the goal-line. This means her footwork has to be good enough and executed early enough to align herself stick to stick with her opponent long before the interception or tackle needs to be made. This leaves apparent space between the opponent and the goal. However it is the stick side of the defender and there are other colleagues already covering for possible danger from this quarter. The left back who allows her opponent to pass her on the non-stick side, letting that inner use the space behind, puts her allies into great difficulty. Whenever the backs alternate roles they must adjust the angle of approaching an opposing player.

An additional job undertaken by the covering back is that of safety net for her ally, the other back. Should the opposing attack pass that player the covering back must be far enough across the field to replace her by forming yet another barrier to be bypassed before the goal circle is reached. Whether she actually moves into the tackle or whether she waits on the circle edge will depend on many factors, the most important being the distance of the play from her defending goal. When play is well away from the defending circle the beaten back will have time and space to recover, so moving into a calculated tackle might be sensible. If the attack is closer to the circle there will be too little time for such a recovery so a waiting position to deny entry into the circle is most efficient.

The key figure in this careful and constant readjustment is the centre-half. By remaining within the central segment of the field she cuts off enough space to make it possible for her other colleagues to close the forward space to the opposing team in possession. She will also be doing her other job of marking the opposing centre-forward or whoever might replace her. Once the centre-half is drawn away from that central area it is not possible for the remaining defenders to close the gaps effectively.

Opinions differ as to the orthodox positioning of the wing halves. Unless there are particular reasons for change the right half is wisest to position nearer to the wing than the inner and near enough to her own goal to be sure that any pass travelling out of reach on her non-stick side must go over the side-line before the opposing wing can reach it. Passes which travel between her and the wing can be intercepted, or failing this, the half is still in a good position to tackle her opponent. The left half need not be so deeply placed since passes to her opposing wing will travel on her stick side. Her problem is to deny the opposition the possibility of using her non-stick side. She does this by playing fairly close to the side-line thus leaving most of the working space on her stick side. Wing halves who place themselves equidistant from the opposing wing and inner forming the apex of a triangle are likely to fail in marking the wing adequately and are likely to muddle their own backs into the bargain. With very careful placing a wing half can mark both the stick and the working space of her opponent.

Whenever a back has to move into a covering position she relies on the adjacent wing half to keep an eye on the opposing inner. If the attack is being mounted in midfield by the opposing left wing, the defending players on that side of the field will be close to their own opponents and the left back will have moved deeper and inwards to cover. The opposing right wing, being furthest from the ball, is least dangerous so the defending left half concerns herself with the space immediately ahead of the opposing right inner. Incidentally, she is still on the pathway of any forward pass to her own opponent, the right wing. As the attack progresses towards the goal circle there is little space to mark and the stick of the right inner is the dangerous problem. So the left half marks that stick closely, being aware of a possible pass to the right wing travelling behind that inner. From her place close to the right inner the left half has the opportunity to anticipate such a pass and intercept it or, failing that, the right wing, having gained possession, is still far enough from the goal circle to be tackled.

Circumstances vary so much that it would be foolish to be dogmatic about who should make that tackle, half or back. If there is time or if the half back has tried and failed to reach the interception she can then give chase to tackle because she has already left the opposing right inner and the left back will have pounced on to her. If, however, the half back continues closely marking the inner it would seem sensible for the back, who has to move from her covering position anyway, to change roles with the half back momentarily and go to tackle the wing. By employing this method the defence denies the opposition that split second when the opposing right inner and wing are unmarked and unharassed whilst two defenders change their places.

Judging when the swing of the backs into covering should begin and when the wing halves should begin to move in is dependent on so many factors that it is impossible to provide an absolutely infallible rule. This knowledge is acquired through match play and full game practice. So long as each defending player knows what she and the whole defending unit aim to achieve she can and must judge each situation afresh. It is vital that she takes into account her own speed relative to that of the opposition and the overall speed of the attack.

So far we have concerned ourselves with detail of general space-marking by the defenders, glossing over what is meant by stick-marking. When play is near or inside the defending circle it is essential that most of the defence ensures that no pass can arrive directly on an opponent's stick. If this is not done the goalkeeper and the covering back, coping with the goalmouth and the space in front of it respectively, will be unable to accomplish their task. To mark an opponent's stick effectively a defender needs to place herself between that opponent and the goal but also nearer to the ball in such a way that the defender will be able to play the ball, should it come, without interference from the opponent. The exact distance must be determined by each individual in that situation, taking into account her own and her opponent's speed off the mark and their distance from the play. Good anticipation of what is likely to occur will be a great asset in refining this judgement.

During all this planning, anticipating and moving the goalkeeper is not idle. She, too, must watch the situation very carefully, covering behind her deep defender at the same time as covering the goalmouth, making sure she never loses sight of the ball, assessing the strength of the attack, anticipating whether it will change from one side to the other, judging which forwards are most dangerous, being ready to cut off a cross-pass travelling close to the goal-line if necessary. Undoubtedly the aims are to start a counter-attack as well as prevent goals but she must remember that the further from the goal-line she waits the more space she leaves behind her un-guarded. Her equipment restricts her from turning quickly and yet she is the only player appropriately dressed to stop shots. No other defending player will aim to do this except in extreme emergency. Instead she will do all she can to restrict the possible angle of shot and to eliminate the opportunity for last-minute passing amongst the opposing attack but she must know she can rely on the goalkeeper to deal with shots.

Constant repetition of the general tactics described for use in attack and defence will obviously lead to stalemate. They need to be known so that they can be used as a base from which players can move unexpectedly and to which they can return for stability between expeditions into the unusual. Defenders base their placing and moving on what they know forwards are likely to do most of the time. In this way they endeavour to block the most obvious routes to goal.

In describing what defenders prefer to do we have, simulta-neously, given all the clues to an opposing attack wishing to penetrate to the goal. As soon as the simple defending strategy is understood, attacking players can create openings without any gross alteration of their orthodox play. From this point the game becomes a battle of wits, a rather rapid game of chess, where those who first discern the failings of the others can deviate from their normal pattern briefly in order to exploit the situation to the full.

Tactical Possibilities in Attack

1. Forwards can move laterally to allow a halfback with the ball to come through and join them, leaving the opposing defence with the problem of six forwards instead of five. Supporting defence players can adjust to replace this halfback by bringing the attack-

ing back to take over her role and making the other halfbacks
cover more deeply and nearer to the centre of the field.

2. A widespread forward line attacking close to the circle edge,
having engaged the attention of the defenders can slip a short
backward pass for the supporting half to collect and shoot.

3. The halfback and the back supporting an attack can follow much
more closely than usual either to preclude any clearance should
the opposing defence steal the ball or to suggest to that defence
that each is ready to become a striking force. The other defenders
of the attacking team will cover more deeply in case the attack
fails.

4. The ball can be lofted into the known spaces in the circle
(provided this is not from a free hit) for a cutting forward to
strike the moment the ball touches the ground.

Creating Attacks from Defence

1. A right wing lying just inside her defending 25 yd. area can collect
a clearance and immediately hit the ball behind the opposing
supporting centre-half to her own left wing lying just inside her
own half, who immediately passes across again while the opposing left back is retreating to cover. The right inner can then
collect the pass close to the attacking 25 yd. line. If either of the
two wings delays the pass by doing any more than controlling
the ball the ploy will probably fail. See Fig. 6.

2. A right back coming through her own defending circle with the
ball can use exactly the same pass to her left wing knowing the
opposing centre-half has not had time to recover from backing
up her attacking forwards.

Foiling a Strong Central Attack

When an attack builds up between inners and centre-forward or
when a breakaway attack develops near the centre of the field the
defending players can make a funnel formation by bringing both
wing halves in close to the inners simultaneously and earlier than
usual. This serves to contain the attack in that central area, forcing
it to meet two successive lines of defence in the shape of the backs
before ever reaching the goalkeeper. In the unlikely event of the

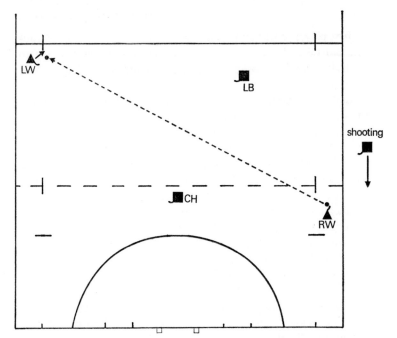

Fig. 6. The long cross-pass to begin an attack from close to the
defending circle

attacking players succeeding in making a pass to either of the unmarked wings, at least the attack will have been forced further away
from goal, giving a little time for the defending team to recover
and cope with a less dangerous situation.

Hunting in pairs can be used by either attacking or defending
players whenever a suitable situation arises. This entails two players
moving one behind the other approximately 3 yd. (2·74 m.) apart.
The first player may be in possession and attempting to dodge the
defender but anticipating that she might not succeed. She completes
her move, whether successful or not, knowing that, should the
defender take the ball, her following ally will be there to dispossess
the defender before she has time to control the ball. The situation
is exactly the same when two defenders take on one attacker in
possession. The first player makes the tackle in such a way that
either she takes the ball or forces the player in possession to dodge
towards the supporting defender who then robs the attacker before
she has time and space to regain full control of the ball. So long as

the first player moves on through the tackle no third-party obstruction can take place. Should the first player stand still or try to tackle back and fail, there is every likelihood that a foul will be committed.

Another useful tactic for any combination of two players against one is that of 'running on'. An opponent in possession is gaining ground, running towards but wide of a colleague. The first player of our tackling pair runs along beside the player in possession on her non-stick side, taking care to be at least two strides clear of her body. She may attempt the occasional jab tackle or she may only look as though she might do so. She certainly makes no attempt to get ahead to make the real tackle. This occupies the attention of the player in possession. She tends to run away from her tormentor and towards our second tackling player who has been momentarily forgotten. This second player waits quite calmly and very easily removes the ball without any foul having taken place.

This same basic idea is often used by a lone right back or right half to encourage the opposing left inner or left wing to run off the goal-line before getting her feet around the ball to centre it or change the direction of her run. The essential factor here is that there should be no suspicion of bodily contact between the attacker and defender running side by side.

Games Within the Game

Like any other game involving large numbers, hockey consists of something more than the one obvious spectacle. It contains a mixture of small units of play happening in relatively small areas ingeniously linked with moves where players far distant from each other are involved in using large parts of the playing area. Thinking only of those immediately concerned with playing the ball causes one to miss one of the most fascinating and necessary aspects of the game. For those well away from current proceedings are busily engaged in playing their own games, which are of real importance to the whole. This is not a ruse to attract straying attention nor should it be so diverting to the players concerned that they lose sight of their place in the total scheme of things. Playing games within the game is the natural extension of sensitivity to all that is happening plus the ability to imagine what could be made to happen from a thorough knowledge of the whole game. These smaller games form the main channels for opening up alternative tactical possibilities.

Any opposition faced with several choices, only one of which will be used, has to make decisions, and therefore has to risk making the wrong guess. If a player in possession is left with only one course of action, her opponents can prepare for this. If her companions are constantly ensuring that she always has a minimum of two possible plays, the opposition has to do more work to block them and is also left uncertain as to which move will be made. The more openings possible for the player in possession, the less able the opponents will be to block them all and the less assured they will feel. Positive pressure of various kinds is being exerted by the whole attacking team. The following examples should help to clarify this assertion that players without the ball make a valuable contribution to the game.

1. Repetition of specific patterns of behaviour can lull the opposition into a sense of security because they feel quite capable of predicting forthcoming events. Once this has been established our team can make a sudden alteration of behaviour which is likely to catch opponents unawares and therefore succeed. It will certainly shake their composure. For instance if a wing or adjacent inner, whichever receives the ball, repeatedly passes to the other, who then returns the pass, the opposing back and halfback will probably cease to try to intercept the first pass or make an immediate tackle. Quite sensibly they will wait for the second pass they know to be coming and steal the ball with little effort. At this point the wing and inner will stop using this repetitive pattern and one of them will sweep forward at speed with the ball having created time and space to do this.

2. Forwards can act as decoys in order to shift opposing players by cutting across in front of a companion in possession. These cuts must be realistically made, and there must be enough space so that no third-party obstruction can take place and the forward concerned must be ready to take the pass just in case. Otherwise the opposing defenders will not be fooled. Supposing the attacking right half who is travelling at speed with the ball finds her inner and wing well marked. The right wing can dart

across towards the inner position looking as though she intends
to receive a short straight pass from the half. What is the opposing left half to do? If the latter goes with the cutting wing she
can foil such a pass but in so doing she leaves a large space
down the non-stick side of her left back and well away from the
latter into which the ball can be placed for the right inner of the
attacking team to collect. This means the defending left half
has been well and truly beaten leaving her defending unit one
player short. If the marking left half does not move with the
attacking right wing, the latter can collect the ball with room
and time to set up other attacking moves. There is no way for that
defending left half to be sure of making the correct decision.
The only player who knows what will happen is the attacking
right half with the ball.

Attacking forwards often find this same cutting by other forwards creates havoc in the opposing defence. In this instance it
may mean the player with the ball has been given a free channel
immediately ahead because a cutting colleague has caused a
defender in that pathway to follow her for a short distance.

3. Immediate passing between two forwards, if it is executed
accurately, is almost impossible for a marking defender to spoil.
This is particularly useful when an attacking team is close to the
shooting circle where it is essential to eliminate one defender
in order to have an unimpaired shot at goal. Supposing the
left inner is approaching the circle with the ball. Her opposing
back will be moving closer to her ready to tackle and the defending centre-half will be marking the attacking centre-forward.
The left inner, just before the back is near enough to interfere,
puts an accurate pass to the centre-forward and keeps running.
The centre-forward immediately taps the ball back for the left
inner to collect directly behind her opposing back for a shot.
Provided the centre-forward makes no attempt to travel with the
ball and is accurate with her pace and placing this tactic rarely
fails. Because the ball is covering such a short distance from inner
to centre-forward it may not need to be controlled but can be
sent straight on without a second's hesitation. This quick timing
of receiving and sending the second pass is vital if the opposing
centre-half is to be denied the opportunity of tackling and if the
attacking left inner is to avoid running the risk of being offside.

4. Because the circle is the most restricted and the most vital area of play it is in this vicinity that most efforts need to be made to shift the opposing defence out of their favourite places. Attacking forwards need space, however little, in which to operate, so defenders will do their utmost to deny them this space. The forwards therefore must use a variety of small games to move the defence or to catch them on the wrong foot. Here are some examples:

(a) Several attackers quite close to the circle or inside the circle can bunch together deliberately in an effort to persuade the defenders marking them to do the same. Yes, this means the defence has the opportunity to keep harassing the attack but it also means each player is too close to another to make a clean tackle or interception and come through with the ball speedily to start a counter-attacking move. Meanwhile at least one of the forwards can be left well away from play, probably unmarked, ready to receive a quick pass from which she can shoot. If the opposing defence refuses this bait the forwards will cease to use it.

(b) The opposite move is also useful. Attackers can pull away laterally or backwards from their colleagues, causing the opposing defenders to go with them if sticks are still to be marked, leaving spaces through which a ball and/or a player can travel. Should the defenders continue to mark the spaces when attackers move away, then the forwards are unmarked for a pass to the stick. One fact is clearly established. No defender is being allowed to mark stick and space simultaneously.

Using a reasonable mixture of drawing together and pulling away the attacking forwards will cause the defenders to worry because they are never sure exactly where a particular opponent may be. It also forces them to be moving slightly most of the time and therefore likely to be caught travelling in the wrong direction. A defence player caught with her weight swaying on to the right foot will find difficulty in changing that weight rapidly enough on to the left foot to make an effective move for the ball.

5. Whenever a forward lies close to the goalkeeper she is a very great danger to the opposing defence as a whole. The offside

rule demanding that two defenders shall be between the player and the goal-line unless she is behind the ball is an asset to the defending team. Thinking forwards can still break through this difficult barrier without attempting to break the rule. If any one of them is prepared to stay in the central area of the goal-circle constantly adjusting her positioning to be perpetually slightly nearer to her own goal than whichever player happens to be the furthest advanced of the two defenders, she will be a positive menace to the opposition for the following reasons:

(a) In order to watch the ball it is most likely that she will have the relevant defenders in her sights so her personal game within the game is easy.

(b) She will engage the attention of the goalkeeper when that player would prefer to have only the play in the immediate vicinity of the ball to watch.

(c) She is likely at times to be too close to the goal-line for her own marking opponent to stay with her without cramping the goalkeeper or blocking her view.

(d) She is ideally positioned for deflecting a cross-pass into the goal with a quick, subtle touch of her stick.

(e) She is beautifully placed to pounce on to the goalkeeper when the latter stops a shot from another attacker. In this way she can either rob the goalkeeper to pop the ball into the net or she can force the goalkeeper into making a hurried inaccurate clearance for another attacking player to take a quick shot.

6. The centre-forward of an attacking team can play a superb game midfield without ever touching the ball. Knowing that it is vital to the opposing defending unit for their centre-half to remain in the central area of the field, the centre-forward can make it her business to shift this opponent. As previously stated the centre-half has two jobs rolled into one: that of marking the attacking centre-forward and of obliterating the space for a pass across the centre of the field. Constantly she has to decide which of these two jobs to do at any given moment. An attacking centre-forward can ensure that these decisions are very difficult to make if she is prepared to employ the following tactics:

(a) By hanging back a little as an attack sweeps towards the goal the centre-forward might lose her marking opponent who goes on blithely expecting that centre-forward to be up with the attack. Result: one free stick in the centre of the field. The defending centre-half may be too wily to be fooled by this move and choose to remain marking her opponent. Result: one space immediately behind that centre-half asking for a ball to be placed into it for any close attacking player to swoop on to.

(b) The centre-forward who bounds up the field well ahead of her own attack, taking care not to be offside, is likely to take the defending centre-half with her. Result: one large space behind the attacking centre-forward for a cross-pass from wing to opposite inner. A defending centre-half who refuses to be drawn in this way risks leaving a dangerous player free to roam laterally to pick up long forward passes without fear of being tackled by her opponent.

(c) By moving laterally either closer to or further away from the inner nearest to the current play the attacking centre-forward hopes to keep the defending centre-half in attendance. Result: an opening in the centre of the field for a cross- or a through-pass. This is particularly useful when the through-pass travels close to the non-stick side of the defending centre-half so that the attacking centre-forward can pounce on to it. The defending centre-half who does not move risks leaving her opponent free once again.

All of these moves are most effective when executed in a fairly small area. The opposing centre-half has to be convinced that the centre-forward making the moves expects to receive the ball. If that player travels far enough to join her own inner the experienced defending centre-half will not worry. She will know that her own back can deal with two players occupying the same space so she will stay in the centre of the field ready to pick up any other attacking player who might decide to replace the centre-forward.

(d) Occasionally a sound defence can be shaken by the centre-forward who moves as if to collect a cross-pass, enticing her defending centre-half to attempt an interception. At the last second the attacking centre-forward lifts her stick allowing the ball to continue. Result: one cross-pass reaching an unmarked inner in spite of the good positioning of the opposing centre-half.

The possibilities described are designed for breaking through a very sound defence. If the opposition is not of sufficient calibre to merit such treatment or if most of the players in the attacking team lack the sensitivity, knowledge and skill to employ such scheming it would be foolish to use it. Cleverness used for its own sake tends to be self-defeating. Nevertheless many opponents are too good to be beaten by employing only the simplest tactics and many teams are fully capable of using ingenuity with skill, deriving great pleasure as well as success thereby. This success can be achieved only when such players are prepared to vary their response to recurrent situations as they arise. Otherwise the whole exciting, exacting process becomes a meaningless mental exercise, a thought or word game quite divorced from its purpose.

Defending players are not barred from using similar games within the game. A halfback positioning to prevent a cross-pass from reaching her opponent can take a small risk to prevent the use of such a pass or to nullify its effectiveness should it be made. Here are some of the possibilities:

(a) A wing half can place herself very slightly further away from her opposing wing than she judges to be best for making an interception. Result: she appears to be blocking all possible forward space so the pass will not be made. However, a pass made to travel behind her and out of her reach will cross the side-line before her opponent can reach it. The hope is that the temptation to place a pass between the wing half and her opposing wing will be too great for the opposition to resist. This will allow the half her usual opportunity to make an interception, knowing that she must start her move earlier and travel faster than usual because she has deliberately increased the distance to be covered. The risk taken is that the halfback will not have sufficient speed to reach this interception but it seems a worthwhile risk to take.

(b) When a defending centre-half decides to employ the same alteration in her positioning exactly the same results are likely except that the ball will not cross the side-line if it passes her, it will travel neatly on to the stick of the covering back. This is particularly useful for preventing or dealing with cross-passes coming from the opposing right-hand side of the field which would travel past the non-stick side of the centre-half.

Obviously, once again, all the players concerned have to be aware of the risks taken and the possible results of their actions. Otherwise the defending team will be playing as a collection of isolated individuals, not as a team at all and any subtle group tactics such as we suggest will prove to be more of a danger than an advantage.

Tactics employed while the ball is moving differ from those used for set-play situations in that they cannot be pre-planned entirely. Though much can be anticipated as a result of knowledge gained from previous matches some adaptation of reactions invariably happens since the same situation rarely recurs exactly. For instance the number of opponents to be beaten, their relative positions and how close to the attacking or defending goal the play happens to be will all vary and will modify the response of the players. The subtle adaptations needed to deal with the immediate situation tax the ability of the players to the full. Indeed they provide much of the excitement of the game and certainly separate the adequate player from the excellent one.

5. *Tactical Possibilities from Set Plays*

THE WORDS 'SET PLAY' refer to the occasions during a game when the ball is 'dead' because it has gone outside the playing area, or because there has been an infringement of the rules, or there has been a stoppage for injury. On such occasions for play to restart the ball must be still—hence the term 'dead'. In all set play situations many of the players need not be still; in fact they should be encouraged to move as we hope to prove by citing the following examples.

The Bully

By design the rules dictate that at this set play both teams shall have equal opportunity of gaining possession of the ball. The major responsibility for success or failure must depend on the skill, perception and ingenuity of the one player from each team designated to take the bully. For our present purposes we must presuppose that any player taking the bully possesses those three attributes to a high degree. The attitude of each team at this situation in the game must be one of determination to start a forceful attack. The very next thought should be 'but we will prepare just in case this is not possible.' The positioning and moves of forwards and defence arise from these two convictions. Similar tactical possibilities will be open whether the bully be taken on the centre-line for starting the match initially and restarting it after each goal or whether it be taken elsewhere on the field because of a simultaneous foul or a stoppage for accidents.

At the start of play the forwards will spread along the centre-line with wings waiting outside the field. This gives maximum width to the playing area. If the feet of the two wings be inside the side-line by only a few centimetres the width of the pitch is reduced by at least half a metre either side, because the ball will never be collected willingly on the toes of the players' boots. The wing need not take up playing space. Only the ball needs to be inside the field. Incidentally, the wing who waits outside the line gives herself maximum opportunity of collecting a hard, diagonal pass into the space ahead of her and simultaneously presents her opponent with more space to cover than is humanly possible. In addition she has increased her chances of cutting in to meet a ball successfully. In fact she has taken every possible advantage of her situation. The moment the bully is complete every forward should anticipate success and move into the territory of the opposition. Occasionally one of the inners may choose to wait behind the centre-line and this tactic is discussed later in the chapter.

With this width of positioning the forward line gives its centre-forward maximum choice of possible tactics when she has obtained the ball. If the opposing defensive unit positions according to the orthodox pattern it will be stretched out laterally leaving large spaces for passes. The centre-forward seeing this will be able to choose from the following courses of action.

(a) Drive the ball hard for a wing, opening up the attack. This is particularly sensible if the pass is sent ahead of her left wing because it is the easy direction for the centre-forward's drive and there will be no opposing back there to restrict the angle of the pass.

(b) Send the ball to an inner. The left inner is the easier choice because she is not closely marked.

(c) Keep the ball herself and accelerate straight towards the goal evading the opposite centre-half and later the right back. These are the only two opposing players near enough to tackle. To use this tactic the centre-forward must be very fast over a long distance. In addition she needs to have her inners coming with her so that the covering back is unsure whether the centre-forward intends to dodge past her or pass to an inner.

There are endless variations on what might happen after any of these initial moves. Some of the best attacks result from the second pass being hit, immediately, hard across the field. This is especially true for the left inner. If she has the stickwork, discipline and timing to receive from the bully, refrain from travelling forwards with the ball, but instead hit it hard at a shallow angle for her right wing so that the opposing defence can be caught completely off balance. The ball should travel between the opposing left back and the centre-line so that the attacking right wing can cut in to collect the ball and head straight for goal. If the drive is timed correctly and placed accurately the opposing centre-half and left back will be in the midst of altering their positioning to cope with an attack building up on their right-hand side. They will be caught at a moment when it is nearly impossible for them to change direction enough to intercept a fast ball travelling on the non-stick side. So two opposing players will have been avoided with one pass. At best this is a tremendous opportunity for an attacking team to reach the shooting circle very quickly with a minimum number of passes. At worst the opposing defence will be shaken out of its composure and, possibly, will have to replan its strategy at a centre bully to prevent such a move being open again. In order to close that particular gap the opposition, having only a limited number of people available, must leave another space open.

The defence of this attacking team following orthodox strategy will position the right half deep and close to the 5 yd. line, the centre-half exactly 5 yd. (4·57 m.) from the bully with her stick directly in line with the ball, the left half less deep but fairly close to the side-line, the right back covering deeply close to the centre of the field, the left back slightly behind and to the left of the centre-half, the goalkeeper a good 6 yd. (5·4 m.) from her goal-line. Plainly the whole defensive unit is ready to give close support to an attack on the left or through the centre of the field. Should the ball travel to the right from the bully it is an easy matter for the right back and right half to move closer to the play while the left back and left half move deeper.

Fortunately this attacking position of the defence at the centre bully is also a sound defensive one. The two wing halves are ready in case a pass is sent to their respective wings. The centre-half is placed ready to block the straight route to goal and the area on her right. The left back is guarding the non-stick side of her centre-half and is in an ideal spot to prevent a pass from reaching her opposing right inner. Clearly the one pass not catered for is that travelling to the opposing left inner. The defence is well aware of this and ready to deal with such an eventuality before an opposing attack could become dangerous. It seems almost as though the defence is begging the opposition to use this pass to start the attack.

Variations on this defensive positioning can be simple and purposeful. The right back can be brought close to the bully instead of the left back if the opposing left inner is deemed to be too dangerous or if the pass from the bully is sent to her frequently. The centre-half can position slightly to one side or other of the central area if she feels this is necessary to cover a potential weakness in her own fielding or to allow for better coverage of the 5 yd. arc around the bully. The wing halves can be brought in closer to the opposing inside forwards should they appear to be very strong, quick and reluctant to feed their own wings.

When a bully has to be taken closer to one side of the field then the forwards rarely alter their positioning materially. The defence usually adjusts in the following way. The wing half, the back on that side of the field and the centre-half form the arc around the bully, the back being more than 5 yd. (4·57 m.) away from it but with her stick in direct line between the ball and the goal-line. To cover for this change in positioning the covering back will move deeper and beyond the centre of the field while the remaining wing half moves deeper and closer to the centre of the field. In this way, once again, a strong attacking and a sound defending unit has been formed.

The Penalty Stroke

The ball is placed 7 yd. (6·40 m.) in front of the centre of the goal-line and the attacker may choose to push, flick or scoop the ball into the net. She may take one step only when the umpire has blown the whistle. The goalkeeper must have her feet touching the goal-line and may not move them until the ball is played. All other rules normally applying to goalkeepers are still in force. Clearly this places the attacker in a very strong position and the goalkeeper in a very weak one, which is exactly what the rule intends.

To gain extra advantage the attacker must disguise her intentions as much as possible until the last second. If she has sufficient strength in her arms she may not need to take the one step allowed which, though it increases her power, also gives the goalkeeper a small chance of guessing her thoughts. The attacker can take up a firm stance with her stick touching the ball ready to send it the moment the whistle blows. All she needs to do is to add power by using a strong thrust from the back foot to propel her body weight into the stroke, produce a whip from the whole trunk and add the quick firm movement of the arms to lift or spin the ball. In this way she will give the goalkeeper no clue as to her intention of which kind of stroke is to be used or the direction in which the ball will travel.

The shots most likely to defeat the goalkeeper are those which are directed to the extreme corners of the goal-mouth at a very fast pace so as to deny her any chance of intercepting the ball. The flick rising to about 6 in. (15 cm.) from the ground is particularly useful because it is harder to judge a ball in the air than a grounded ball; because the spinning ball travels faster and tends to be deflected when stick or pads touch it rather than rebound from them; because it is nowhere near high enough for the hand to be used to stop it. If the goalkeeper is short it might be sensible to use the fling stroke to place the ball just inside the top corner of the goal-posts to the right of the goalkeeper. This will be well above the hand of the goalkeeper trying to save it. There is also the possibility that a goalkeeper having to react at such speed will forget to transfer her stick from the right hand and reach to the ball with it or even drop her stick in an effort to transfer it. In either case a penalty goal would be awarded.

Some general useful advice when taking a penalty stroke would be: vary the height and direction of the shot; prey on the known weaknesses of the goalkeeper; appear confident when approaching the ball; take time to prepare the best stance and take a deep breath to ensure calmness and concentration. It would be a pity to waste such a golden opportunity by making avoidable errors.

The goalkeeper is in a very serious situation but must be determined to come out of it successfully. Initial positioning will vary with each individual. If the goalkeeper stands with her toes touching the back edge of the goal-line she has increased her distance from the ball and therefore her reaction time as much as possible, but she has taken the risk that the ball may be wholly over the line when it touches her pads. Should she decide to position with her heels touching the front edge of the goal-line she has narrowed the angle for shooting as much as possible but has also reduced her reaction time to the minimum. A stance with the heels touching the back edge of the goal-line seems to produce the best results. Most women find that the amount the shooting angle can be reduced by being farther forward is too small to compensate for the loss of reaction time and the extra distance gained by standing farther back increases the time too little to be effective. Where and how to hold the stick is another problem that has to be solved. If it is held as usual in the right hand it can increase the goalkeeper's reach to that side but it prevents her from releasing the right hand quickly to stop a high ball. If she holds it in the left hand it is virtually useless as the back of the stick will be presented to the ball and that is a foul. The best position then would seem to be that of gripping the stick loosely with both hands, keeping it parallel to the ground. From here it is easy for either hand to be released or for the stick to be thrust quickly through the right-hand grip by the left hand to its full extent.

To give herself the best opportunity of saving the shot the goalkeeper must be poised and ready to move in any direction, looking large, alert and aggressive. If she is particularly quick at moving to her right she might position a little to the left of centre on the goal-line. This could tempt the opponent into placing the ball in an area which looks larger but which the goalkeeper knows she is capable of covering. She must watch the feet and stick of the attacker very closely indeed in case these provide a clue to the shot which is to follow. Knowing that the opponent has a powerful shot may cause the goalkeeper to take the calculated risk of diving to one side as the ball is played, hoping that she has chosen the correct side. With a little courage the goalkeeper could attempt to distract the attacking player by moving her body before the ball is played. Though she may not move her feet there is no reason why she should not feign a move in the hope of causing the opponent to change her predetermined stroke at the last minute thereby producing a less efficient shot. If, by her attitude and precision of positioning, she can create the impression that scoring will not be easy the goalkeeper will have done all that is possible in this extremely difficult situation.

The Push-in

This could be regarded as a similar situation to the taking of a free
hit except that it is even more restricted. The side-line precludes
the use of space behind the player with the ball and only one method
of propulsion, the push, is allowed so the ball must stay on the
ground. The player taking the push stands with the ball on the
line and her stick very obviously in contact with the ball since there
must be no suspicion of a striking action being used. All other
players must be at least 5 yd. (4·57 m.) away but they are no longer
pinned behind a 5 yd. (4·57 m.) strip of the whole field. Most frequently this leads to the opposition making a ring around the ball,
using their sticks to sweep the ground, creating what they hope will
be an impenetrable barrier. Quite often this proves to be the case.
Disguising the direction of the push cannot be effective if all
escape-routes are covered. Therefore it is imperative that the push
should be taken too quickly for such a barrier to be formed. If this
is not possible then many tactics which are described for use at a
free hit might be effective here.

It is useful to remember that players waiting to receive the ball
can position outside the side-line ahead of and behind the player in
possession ready for the ball pushed along the line. The player in
possession has no restriction placed on where her feet must be. So
long as the ball is on the line her feet can be outside or inside the
field of play. Understanding this is invaluable to a player taking the
push on the left-hand side of the field. By stepping round the ball
quickly into the field she can push the ball along the line to a
colleague waiting outside the line nearer to her defending goal than
the ball. That player is less likely to be marked than those who are
ahead of the ball.

Once the ball has been moved all players are able to enter the
restricted area so a gentle push could be used for a team-mate to
dash on to and drive or lift the ball through the barrier of opposing
sticks. Variations on this particular use of accurate knowledge of
the rule are endless and are very effective if executed decisively.

A particularly effective ruse on the right-hand side of the field
involves using a quick backward pass. Suppose the right half
takes the push along the line to the right wing who is outside it,

nearer to her attacking goal and closely marked by her opponent. If the right wing has the wit to meet the ball quickly, without obstructing her opponent and push the ball diagonally back to the right half, who will have moved into the field of play, the half can then drive the ball hard across the pitch thus avoiding the knot of opposing players.

Occasionally the opportunity may arise to send the ball directly to the middle of the field from a push-in. If the pass can be taken quickly enough and with a lot of power the ball can reach a wise centre-forward or centre-half hovering free in that large space ready for such a chance. When placing the ball for the push-in a player should check to see if this pass is possible for it will remove the ball from a tight mass of players and allow the attack to be mounted quickly from an unexpected quarter.

Accuracy of stroke production is of very great importance if the push-in is to prove the advantage it is supposed to be. Too much haste can result in careless manipulation of the stick. So often the left hand is jerked back in an effort to add power. This will make the ball rise and that is not allowed. Care, courage and celerity are the key words for success in this situation.

Free Hits and The Hit-out

The unbeatable tactic in this situation on whatever part of the field the ball may be is for it to be placed and sent very quickly and accurately. The player nearest to the ball should take the hit in order to achieve this result. We have presupposed that all players in the newly attacking team will react as quickly as the one taking the hit. If this can be done no special tactics are needed because the opposing team will have had no time to form a special barrier. For the occasions when such speed is not possible some thought has to be given to retaining possession. It is important that players hoping to receive the ball do not choose a spot on the field and stay there regardless of their opposition. A moving player is harder to mark. A moving player finds it easier to collect a ball than one whose feet are firmly planted when the ball arrives.

During most of a match all attacking players should be trying to create space through which the ball can travel, or presenting a free stick to their own player taking the hit. To achieve either of these results a player may need to make several moves in a short space of time or she may need to draw slowly away from the vicinity of the ball in order to make a very sudden dart into the space she has created. As in normal passing during the run of play the position of an attacking player at a free hit relative to her opponent sends messages to the colleague with the ball. For instance, a wing lying close to her opponent and close to the ball is asking for the pass to be sent well ahead through the space created behind that opponent. If she lies close to her opponent but well away from the ball she is expecting to run back to collect a short pass. The inner who draws her opponent towards another of her companions is asking for the ball to be sent through that large space for any one of her allies to collect.

In midfield these possibilities are easy to see because they relate so closely to normal play. Free hits awarded close to the attacking circle need special thought because of the comparative lack of area and the quantity of defenders. At such a time wings who move out to the side-line are worth their weight in gold. They either spread out the defence leaving valuable spaces or they present an unmarked stick. Supposing one of the wing halves has the free hit. As she is placing the ball she must check whether any forward is in the circle free to receive a pass. If this is the case all her troubles are over and the hit can be made almost before she has regained her upright position. Failing this she can expect:

(a) her nearby wing to draw out to the side-line ready for one of the passes described above;

(b) her inside forwards to advance into the circle taking their opponents with them creating space behind themselves;

(c) the wing on the opposite side of the field to move out towards the side-line and slightly behind the level of the ball ready for a hard square pass;

(d) her supporting back to be behind her for a short backward pass.

From these possibilities she must select the pass most likely to get the ball into the circle most quickly. If too many passes have to travel around the circle, there is less likelihood of the ball ever getting through at all. As variations on this free hit, the wing could become the striker, thereby adding to the list of possibilities that of using a backward pass to the half who can then distribute play or move into the circle with the ball.

When the attacking centre-half has to take a free hit just outside the circle edge she is even more dependent on the movement of the forwards to help her. Using a pass for a free wing is not as foolish as it may sound. Although the ball has travelled further away from the goal-mouth it is often possible to make that ball cut the circle edge far out to the side at exactly the same moment as the free wing arrives to strike it and before the opposing defence can rearrange themselves to tackle. The opportunity every centre-half in this situation seeks is to place the ball so that its speed is dying as it arrives in the space between the stick-marking defenders and the space-marking defender. It is rarely seen but can be made possible if the left inner moves back towards the circle edge bringing her opponent with her, the right inner draws forward and out to the right, and the centre-forward moves slightly to the left taking the opposing centre-half out of the line of the ball. The centre-forward or the right inner can then race on to that loose ball to her team's immense satisfaction.

The most difficult free hit to be taken in the defensive area of the field is that awarded as a result of a foul committed by an opposing player striking a corner hit. Fortunately this happens rarely. Unless the free hit from this spot on the defending goal-line can be taken quickly it proves to be more of a disadvantage than an advantage. Supporting forwards must be prepared to move to the 5 yd. limit allowed and then be ready to meet a short tap by the player taking the hit or receive a square pass travelling towards the side-line. Great skill and accuracy are required by all players concerned.

Free hits awarded in the defending quarter of the field near the 5 yd. line stand a reasonable chance of success if any of the general tactics previously described are employed. It is worth remembering that hits awarded in the defending circle can be taken from any spot within that circle. Sometimes it will be expedient for the hitter to strike the ball from a spot well inside the circle so that it can be sent on its way quickly. At other times it might be wiser to place the ball on the circle edge so as to gain as much ground as possible. On other occasions it will be sensible for the defence to send the ball rapidly across the circle so that a defender may take the hit well away from the main grouping of opposing players.

When the back is taking a hit from the circle edge in addition to the movements of forwards suggested earlier for other free hits, she needs the aid of her nearby wing half and centre-half. Their way of helping is to position well away from the back laterally and at least two strides behind the level of the ball. In so doing the wing half allows the back the opportunity to give her a square pass while the centre-half removes herself from the pathway of a pass travelling diagonally across the field. One is told very early in a hockey-playing career never to pass across one's defending circle. Nevertheless, such a pass can be most effective (particularly for the right back) provided that it is not used too frequently. The opposing centre-half very often draws slightly towards the side of the field from which the hit is to be taken leaving a gap to the left inner of the team in possession, whose opponent is covering deeply at the time.

If the opposing team has had time to settle itself it may push several forwards close to the back taking the free hit and place its defenders to mark any spaces left by the forwards. Details of this defensive move will be covered later in the chapter. Should this happen the forwards trying to retain possession need to be very crafty and active. One of them can place herself on the stick side of an opposing forward, who is exactly 5 yd. (4·57 m.) from the hit, ready to do one of two things. She can either reach back to collect a gentle hit before the opposing forward can touch it or she can deflect the ball that is hit hard directly towards that opposing player. Meanwhile another attacking forward can run through the arc formed by the opposing forwards acting as a decoy to distract their attention or to collect a short hit as she runs. The back still has the possibility of using the backward wing half and she still has the opportunity to drive the ball very fast through a gap left by the opposing forwards. The sheer pace of the hit often defeats their vigilance. Now that the rules allow the ball to be off the ground from a free hit there is an added possibility for the player taking it. A strong disguised flick making the ball pass the knot of opposing forwards at knee height will be very difficult for them to stop. A high scoop from this situation is less likely to succeed. There is too little working space to ensure that the ball will not be dangerous.

All tactics which are viable for a free hit from the circle edge are available to the player taking a hit-out from a very slightly altered position. The hit-out taken by the half back nearer to the side-line can utilize the tactics suggested for free hits from a similar spot. In both instances the goalkeeper nearby can assist greatly if she fields the ball just after it crosses the goal-line and sends it to the exact spot from which the hit-out must be taken. Her speed in doing this may enable the hit to be taken too quickly for complex tactics to be necessary.

At a free hit or hit-out the newly defending team (that is, the team just relinquishing possession) should be determined to regain it immediately. Assuming this aim to be established in a player's mind we must consider how best to achieve it. Speed of repositioning is a prime factor. Without this all hope of stealing the ball is gone. Some players with a real flair for the game seem to know, as if by instinct, where the hit will be sent and get themselves into line with it. Such individuals barely consider consciously why they move where they move. However, not every team is fortunate enough to contain players with this attribute so it is useful to consider team efforts which are likely to succeed in regaining the ball.

The most obvious tactic is the simplest. It reflects normal playing positions and it succeeds with amazing regularity. The players in the defending team, that is the team not currently in possession, add their forwards into the usual marking system, for example the wing marks the stick of the opposing wing. This means the defenders continue to mark the spaces while the nearby forwards attach themselves to their opposing forwards. Let us suppose a left back has been awarded a free hit close to the centre-line and the ball was rather slow in reaching her. The left wing, left inner and centre-forward on her team will be moving to become free and to leave spaces. Our defending right wing calmly attaches herself to the stick of that left wing and moves with her. Our defending right inner follows the same limpet-like procedure with the opposing left inner and our centre-forward picks up her opposite number. Result: no sticks free to receive the free hit.

Now to deal with the spaces. Once the defending right back, right half and centre-half know that the attacking forwards are closely marked they can concentrate entirely on positioning to cover the spaces. These spaces will form one channel to the centre of the field, another straight ahead of the ball, and another diagonally to the side of the field. They may change slightly as the attacking forwards move about, but a couple of strides to one side or the other by any one of the three close defenders will deal with each changing situation. The picture created for the left back taking the hit is one of apparent space and great activity. Yet every space has a smiling opponent at the end of it while all the activity seems to be of no avail. The defending team has probably succeeded in doing one of two things: either it has tempted the right back into using one of the apparent spaces where the defender is ready to collect the ball, or it has forced her into using a complex tactic which is more likely to fail and at best neither gains ground nor eliminates an opponent.

Forming a 'ring' around the player taking the free hit can be very useful if those concerned have sufficient self-discipline to form it quickly and accurately. An incomplete or inaccurate 'ring' is a waste of time and energy. It can be a most effective tactic against a hit-out where there is little space for backward passing. For example, the right back is taking the hit from 4 or 5 yd. (3·66 or 4·57 m.) beyond the line of the right-hand goal-post. The defending left wing, left inner, centre-forward and right inner rush towards her, forming an arc in front of her exactly 5 yd. (4·57 m.) away from the ball. There will be a space of about 2 yd. (1·83 m.) between each of these forwards guarded by the left half, left back and centre-half. Results:

(a) the right back can barely see the rest of the field because of the bodies forming the 'ring';
(b) there is no hope of a cross-pass to her left inner because the arc of four players brings the two outermost defending forwards almost level with the ball;
(c) the pass to her right half is doubtful for the same reason;
(d) there is very little space between the bodies in the arc through which to flick or drive the ball;
(e) the right back is in trouble.

A 'ring' can consist of only three of the defending forwards. It does save a little energy if the defending right inner need not hurtle across the field for every free hit on that side. At times by dropping back and towards the centre of the field, almost in the centre-forward's normal spot, the right inner can be just as effective as by adding herself to the 'ring'. She is still in a position to cut off a shallow cross-pass and she might have tempted the hitter to use the apparent gap left in the 'ring' by her absence. The real repercussions of reducing the number of players in the arc are felt by the defenders marking the spaces behind the arc. Three people instead of four must either leave more space between each other if they wish to complete a semicircle of 5 yd. (4·57 m.) radius or they must cover less of the arc. Whichever they choose to do, more spaces are left for their defenders to block.

The free hit and the hit-out are the most frequently recurring set play situations in the game. Consequently the few examples given here are not intended to be a complete list of possibilities but they should provide a sound basis for invention. New variations are appearing every season. From these the wise coach or player will select the best to add to her repertoire.

The Attacking Corner

This is virtually a free hit to the attacking team with added advantages to them. The rules do all in their power to prevent the opposing players from impeding the progress of this hit to an attacker in the shooting circle. The attacking team should be skilful and sensible enough to make the most of this opportunity. A hard ball struck forcibly can travel faster than can any human being, starting from a stationary position. Without any knowledge of hockey a reasoning person would assume that, under these circumstances, a ball hit accurately could be stopped and hit again long before an opponent could interfere. Those who know hockey realize that it is not quite so simple because the reach of a running defender with a stick in the hand reduces the distance to be covered considerably. In addition, the spot from which the ball must be hit predetermines the angles at which the ball can be sent and the distance it has to travel. Having taken these factors into account the most useful corner hit in most cases is that which travels fast, without bouncing, to the stick of the recipient on the inside edge of the circle directly in front of the goal. The shooting player then has the maximum time for the shot plus maximum choice of angles for placing the ball around the goalkeeper.

Before we consider adaptations let us first determine what is required of the receiving players irrespective of the tactics to be employed. According to the rules, they must be outside the circle until the ball has been hit and they must stop it before they can shoot. Those are the only added restrictions imposed by the corner rules. In order to effect a quick shot each waiting player should arrange herself so that the ball will be on the circle-line when she stops it thus giving herself maximum time to shoot because she has not reduced the distance the defenders have to run in order to tackle her. She should ensure that her left shoulder points towards a space in the goal-mouth and also her right foot so that, having trapped the ball, she can step into the shot quickly and easily, whether it be a drive, a flick, a scoop or a push. From such a position she is ideally situated should the ball be badly hit and arrive 1 yd. (0·91 m.) or so inside the circle. Her feet are ready to run towards it and use it immediately. Should the ball be fumbled slightly by the receiving player she can still manage a hard shot off the right foot, provided her head is over the ball at the moment of striking. Ideally the player should trap the ball an optimum distance away from her own feet so that no adjustments of body or feet need to be made after the ball has arrived. She must ensure that the blade of her stick is exactly at right angles to the line of the ball and that her grip is relaxed enough to cushion the impact of ball on stick. When the ball is coming from her left she must be quite happy to have her back to it with only her head watching its movement closely, knowing that she will allow it to pass across in front of her feet to reach her waiting stick. Alternatively she could reach towards the ball with her stick to take some of the pace from it as ball and stick continue together to her stick side. The corner hit coming from the right should be received well away from the feet with the stick blade ensuring that any accidental rebound will neither travel across to the non-stick side nor allow the ball to land on her toes. Unless she is the furthermost player on the circle edge any corner hit travelling to her non-stick side is not intended for her but for her neighbour, so she should refrain from interfering. The attacking half backs will always be there to handle any mistaken hit or failure to field the ball. In addition to these practical adjustments a player waiting to receive a corner hit must notice the relative speed, reach and strength of her particular opponent, the accuracy of the positioning of all defenders and the weaknesses of the goalkeeper. This will allow her the opportunity to select the placing and kind of shot with deadly accuracy. For instance, goalkeepers tend to have poorer reach and stopping power in the left foot, therefore it is sensible to aim for that side. They tend to dislike a ball travelling at knee height, therefore a strong flick is useful. Those who move well into the circle from the goal-line are imploring attackers to use a high scoop shot. At all times the receiving player should concentrate on the angle and the type of shot that she is to make. It is imperative that some kind of shot be made, avoiding the legs of the approaching defence, if the simple corner is to be effective. Even if the shot is not particularly good, at least it can be regarded as the best forward pass for other attackers to pounce on. Certainly the pressure has been forced on to the defending team to clear the ball out of the danger area.

By stressing the recipient first we have given some very clear indications as to the role of the player taking the corner hit. For her accuracy is paramount. She must know exactly where the ball must first cut the arc of the circle in order to arrive at its destination and must make it do so regularly. This is especially true at a corner (long) as opposed to a penalty corner (short) where the distance which the ball has to travel will exaggerate any inaccuracy. Because, as in any kind of pass, she has the receiver in mind, the hitter must make the ball travel crisply and flat enough to be received easily yet fast, and far enough to reach the attacking player long before the opposing defence can arrive to tackle. She can take all the time she needs to prepare for her hit. She can be sure the ball rests on a level piece of ground provided it is still on the line, without infringing the distance limits set by the rules. She can adjust her footwork with no pressure from the opposition and so produce a copy-book stroke. Usually she will choose to use a drive and may well need to exaggerate the extension of the follow-through in order to keep the ball flat (i.e., travelling without bouncing) over a long distance. The hitter may decide to prepare for her drive keeping her stick lifted away from the ball ready to strike. In this way the opposing defence will have no guide to the rhythm of her swing and a very much shorter time in which to determine her moment of impact for their initial surge over the goal-line. She may also choose to use a grip with both hands well down the handle of the stick to prevent too high a backlift and at the same time add extra power to her hit. The moment the ball has been struck she must move very fast indeed directly towards the centre-line, not towards the goal-mouth, in order to avoid being caught offside. Alternatively she could step well behind the boundary-line but will then be unable to take any further part in the game until the play is well away from her. The latter is not normally the best procedure for it seems a pity to reduce the number of players on a team voluntarily, except in unusual circumstances, and she may be ruled offside.

The fast accurate corner hit which is stopped cleanly, followed by a quick shot, will defeat most defenders. The rules do not dictate which players must take the hit nor which players may receive, so the team in possession can always choose from its players those most capable of doing so. The remaining attacking players can be ready to follow up the shot, retrieving rebounds, deflections or attempts to clear the ball away from goal.

Adaptations

There are times when other tactics may need to be employed in order to make the corner hit succeed. If the opposing defence is particularly fast and particularly sound, some means of out-thinking them must be found. Certainly any attacking team repeatedly failing to convert a corner into a goal, or at least a shot, needs to try some alternative ploys until a successful one is found.

1. One of the simplest variations for a corner (long), infrequently used but with a fair chance of success, is for the hit to be taken from 5 yd. (4·57 m.) up the side-line. Some people favour this from the right; we favour it from the left for the following reasons:

   (a) The pathway of the ball is never close to the opposing defence.
   (b) The ball travelling towards the left inner position from this angle, if it is missed by the nearest player, passes easily on to the next and yet a third player on the circle edge with very little adjustment of their positioning. Therefore three successive players have had the chance of trapping the ball.
   (c) The opposing defence will not know which of the three forwards intends to stop the ball and shoot.
   (d) It is more difficult for the opposing defence to intercept a ball coming from their right.
   (e) The hitter is less likely to be caught offside.

2. At a penalty corner the rules allow the attacking team to choose

from which side of the field the hit shall be taken. This can give some advantage to the attacking team which notes whether the opposing defence on the right is faster off the goal-line than the defenders on the left. They will avoid taking the hit where the defenders are faster. It may be that the receiving attacking players have a particular preference for collecting a ball from the left. The goalkeeper may leave more goal-mouth unguarded when she covers for shots from the attacking left. On the other hand all these might be equal. This being so, the corner hit travelling from the attacking left will still cause the opposing defence to attempt a most difficult interception.

3. Though the high controlled scoop has become fashionable again in general play it has not been revived as a shot following a corner hit. Some years ago it was used consistently with great success. Granted it requires hard regular practice, but what skill does not? At present goalkeepers are tending to position well in front of the goal-line so this would be an ideal moment for players of skill and courage to resurrect this high scoop shot. As in most cases the initial corner hit needs to be crisp and accurate and the ball must be trapped cleanly by the recipient to give herself maximum time to prepare for a stroke that will lift the ball very high very quickly. The player producing this strong throwing action should have ample time to change her grip if she prefers to place her left hand down the stick in order to produce greater accuracy. Care must be taken to ensure that the ball is not propelled into the advancing defenders as it rises. It should aim to drop just under the cross-bar of the goal in the centre where it will be out of reach of any backs who may be covering the corners of the goal-mouth and in the most difficult position for a retreating goalkeeper to make contact.

4. Many variations in the personnel waiting to receive can be used. Halfbacks or backs can replace forwards on the circle edge for the duration of the corner. This is especially sensible if any of them has a particularly hard shot. The opposing defence will note this and make a special effort to reach that unusual player before she can shoot. This may well mean a little less accuracy in their coverage of other players. Should this happen the attacking team can either use that player to receive or keep her there on the circle edge as a decoy and send the corner hit to a forward

E

left loosely marked. Defence players can be used to add to the usual four players on the circle edge so that the opposition has to make a rapid readjustment to deal with the extra possible striker. Alternatively the arrangement around the circle can look highly orthodox with its usual four forwards on the edge and the halfbacks in the normal backing-up capacity, but one half-back is going to move into the space between two forwards as the corner hit is taken, becoming a surprise fifth player ready to receive the ball and shoot unmolested.

5. The tactic of using a supporting wing half who is not on the circle edge at a corner (long) to receive the hit unmolested and then either travel in to shoot or make a quick cross-field pass is a fairly popular one and can be effective. In using this ploy the attacking team must realize the risks it is taking:
   (a) the ball still has to get into the circle;
   (b) no defenders have been eliminated;
   (c) two passes are likely to take longer than one in order to get the ball into a shooting position;
   (d) the initial hit is travelling away from the goal-mouth;
   (e) there is no player backing up the wing half should she fail to stop the ball.

   Even so the attacking team does have the chance to alter rapidly the area from which the attack will come, causing the opposing defence a good deal of trouble!

6. Altering the placing of attacking players around the circle edge leads to countless possibilities for unsettling an opposing defence. Whenever anything looking unorthodox arises that poor defence has to assume that something unusual is about to happen and plan for it. Whether the unusual event is actually to take place only the attacking team knows. Often these odd arrangements are very useful as a decoy so long as they are realistic in their placing.

   The normal placing of attackers around the circle edge—well-spaced, with one player as near to the hit as possible, still leaving a shooting angle available—is very sensible. For instance, at a penalty corner, the nearest recipient can be exactly opposite to the ball placed 10 yd. (9·14 m.) from the goal-post on the goal-line and still have a very good shooting angle. The hit can then travel the shortest distance, a straight line, forming the short side of a triangle. Meanwhile, the 5 yd. (4·57 m.) distance, that the nearest defender must allow as she waits for the corner hit to be struck, forms another short side to the triangle. As that defender runs out to tackle she must travel a comparatively long distance along the third and long side of the triangle. This even spacing gives the recipients ample room to manoeuvre once the ball arrives; the opportunity to recover should the hit or the fielding be slightly less than accurate; the chance to pass accurately should this be necessary; and good coverage of the whole circle area when following up a shot. All these advantages accrue because, in spacing themselves well apart, the receivers have made it necessary for the opposing defenders to spread out evenly if they are to tackle or mark thus leaving working spaces for ball and/or attackers to use. This simple, orthodox arrangement is useful when the opposition demands nothing more complex, or when no previous decision has been made as to who will receive the hit. The major disadvantage of using this ploy is the predictability of it. The opposition knows well in advance the possible results and has arranged itself in a very organized orthodox fashion to cover for these.

With a little pre-match planning and practice, several simple surprises can be used. When a corner hit is being taken from the attacking left-hand side of the field this is one effective tactic for the recipients to gain some element of surprise in this most orthodox of placing. It is based on the knowledge that each opposing defender will have settled herself opposite her own opponent ready to run the shortest possible distance. Having done this, she must then watch the ball only so as to time her move into the field of play. If, as the striker's stick drops to hit the ball, each receiver moves one large stride to her right each defender will be caught hurtling towards the space on the non-stick side of her opponent, exactly where she would least like to be. There is too little time for the defender to change course sufficiently to put herself in a healthy position to tackle. So that this ploy may succeed, the player striking the corner hit must be sure to direct the ball to the space between two of her colleagues on the circle edge at their initial line-up. Their one step will bring them to the exact spot when the ball arrives.

7. Another possible tactical move for the corner taken from the left has proved most effective if used infrequently. It is based on

noting that the opposing defence is very fast off the goal-line and very accurate in its group positioning. By placing the attacking right wing only 4 yd. (3·66 m.) from the goal-line on her patch of the circle edge, the hit can be sent very hard at a very acute angle. It needs to pass between the positions habitually occupied by the covering back and the goalkeeper. The sheer pace of the hit as well as the unusual direction frequently beats the goalkeeper who is the only defender able to intercept safely. The reasons for using such a hit are quite sound. The attacking right wing is furthest from the hit and would therefore normally be left free by the opposing defence. The goalkeeper is usually covering the goal-mouth to her right of centre and has therefore left extra space on her left. All the opposing defence have to arrest their rapid running and recover to reach the ball side of their respective opponents. In fact, the opposition has been presented with a very difficult task, provided that the initial hit is deadly accurate.

8. An attacking team fortunate enough to possess a centre-half who is able to take a quick, hard shot might make the most of her prowess during a corner hit taken from the attacking left. If the centre-forward positions herself to the left of centre she can receive and control the ball, send it gently a few yards to her right, parallel to the goal-line, for her centre-half to move in at speed to take an immediate shot. Two important points must be noted if this ploy is to be a success. The initial corner hit must be controlled before the short pass is made and the centre-half must start in her normal supporting role behind the centre-forward. If the former is not done the rules will have been broken and if the latter is not done there will be no space in which to place the ball. Should the centre-half be tempted to anticipate her move towards the crown of the circle and move too soon the opposing defence will most likely detail a player to rush towards that spot. The beauty of such a shot lies in the fact that the ball will have been placed to the non-stick side of the opposing centre-half and yet be out of reach of the left half who has rushed out to mark the right inner. Because the attacking centre-half is shooting on the run, her drive is likely to be very powerful and her own impetus can carry her on to follow up the shot.

9. One of the wildest possibilities of regrouping forwards in the hope of creating confusion in the opposing defensive ranks is to present apparent confusion to them. The attacking players concerned in the corner hit must know beforehand which of them is to receive the ball and where she will be to trap it. Then, as opposition and hitter arrange themselves for the corner, all the other attacking players concerned dart hither and thither for a very short time until the one designated to receive moves decisively to the predetermined spot on the circle edge. At this moment the hitter strikes the ball and all becomes settled and normal. This has been known to work very effectively against defenders who slavishly try to find their own particular opponent to tackle willy-nilly. One thing is certain, no defender can have the smallest idea whence the shot will eventually be made. Naturally where such close co-operation and split-second timing are demanded from the attacking team this tactic is open to error. Without accuracy it can be a complete waste of effort.

10. The most obvious grouping of attackers on the circle edge occurs when the corner hit is to be stopped by the hand of one player for a second player to strike. The two recipients concerned will work very close together: the striker with her stick lifted ready to drive, the stopper crouching (or ready to) with her body well away from the body of the striker. Once the ball has arrived the stopper should need only to sway backwards as she lifts her hand from the ball. From such a position she will also be ready to move away rapidly before the ball arrives should the corner hit be bouncy or inaccurate in its direction, giving her colleague room to receive the ball in the usual way. The great advantage of the hand-stop is that it cuts down the time needed for trapping and driving the ball. The striker can make her preparatory backlift before the corner hit is taken instead of after the ball has arrived. She can also concentrate on getting maximum power behind her drive. The disadvantages are that, if the ball is fumbled, however slightly, by the hand of the stopper, a free hit will be awarded to the opposition; and that the opposing defence knows in advance what is to happen and can arrange to deal with this.

11. Other groupings on the circle edge aim to increase the space between possible recipients. It is hoped this will spread the

opposing defence more widely, creating greater space for a
pass after the corner hit has been received, or for a supporting
half back to move into in order to receive the initial corner hit.
For instance, a wing half could strike the corner hit leaving
five forwards to receive, two of whom will be close to the left
of the circle and the other three will be huddling together
over on the right of it. As usual the opposition will not know
towards which group the hit will travel, but, in addition they
will not know which player in the group will take the shot. If
three of the defence rush out to the three snuggling forwards,
they will find themselves too close to each other to manoeuvre
efficiently so a muddle is likely to ensue. The defence also has
the added problem of what to do about the large space in the
centre of the circle apparently devoid of attacking players.
After all the receiving player, having stopped the ball, could
easily send a gentle square pass towards the crown of the circle
for the supporting centre-half to move into at speed and shoot
immediately. In this way their mental and physical resources
will be stretched. Varying the place of the groupings or the
numbers involved in each cluster, leaving one lone player
isolated, are obvious variations on this tactic, all aiming to
achieve the same results: that is, working space and uncertainty
in the opposition.

Perhaps these suggestions will serve to help players and coaches to
invent other tactical possibilities. Nothing is certain of success so
variations are worth trying. There is no substitute for the skill
and accuracy needed for making corner hits effective. The more
complex the tactic the more demanding it is of all those involved
and the greater the possibility of error. Whenever preplanned
tactics are in operation at corner hits or at any other time, the same
dangers are present. Each player concerned knows her own predetermined role and is ready to play it, but she is likely to be less
able to adapt should plans go awry. In addition, her peripheral concentration may be diminished because all her mind is centred on the
one known job in hand. This, too, leads to reduced spontaneous
reaction when mistakes occur.

Defending at a Corner

It might seem as though the award of a corner hit to an attacking team spells imminent doom to the defending team. This should be the case but we all know it is not so. Sensible, calm, disciplined defending can minimize and often nullify the advantages given to attacking players. If every defender knows her own role and has a clear understanding of the defensive unit as a whole, then she can be ready to play a full part in this rapid battle of skill and wit. She can adapt quickly should that be necessary or play her anticipated part in the encounter. Panic is the defender's worst enemy. Hesitancy runs it a very close second. To assess and act decisively is imperative. The attack intends to offer all kinds of problems and temptations. The defence has to determine which offers are worth buying. Several of the problems set by attacking players at corners have in mind the same objectives so that, once these are diagnosed, the treatment for them can be prescribed easily. The defending unit that plans to deal with the obvious danger confronting it but also refuses to place all its powers in the one area is likely to succeed. Life cannot be easy in this situation for any defender but she must make it as easy for herself as possible and as difficult as she can for the opposing attack.

A few basic disciplines are necessary whatever tactics are being employed. All the defenders designated to mark the sticks of the opposing attacking players must aim to be close to those sticks before the ball travelling from the corner hit can arrive. To do this they must position themselves behind the goal-line so that their run shall be the shortest distance. They must make the pathway of the run at right angles to the goal-line, to the stick side of the opponent not towards her body. In this way the legs of the defending players will not be between the shooting player and the goal, and the tackle that may be made will be as easy as possible for the defender. The latter must also ensure that she can see the player striking the corner hit in order to time her tremendous sprint start. This may mean that she has to be upright with all her weight on the back foot, or it may be that she has to crouch very low over her front foot so that she does not allow the bodies of the other defenders to obstruct her view.

It is essential that, whatever the conditions of the ground, every defender has a very strong stable base so that her initial thrust away from the area behind the line is good. She must experiment with her waiting stance, sometimes having her feet wide apart, sometimes keeping the feet fairly close together until she finds which foot positions give her the stability she seeks. It may be that she has to turn sideways to the goal-line and dig into the ground with the inside and outside edges of her feet. Somehow, she has to find a powerful grip. Finally, she must discipline herself to run most of the distance from goal-line to circle edge with her stick sweeping the ground before her and with two hands holding it. Only then is she a menacing player. The speed of her travelling, the strength in her stick and the extent to which that stick blocks a possible shot at goal combine to put great pressure on the attacking player expecting to receive the ball.

Imagine yourself as a forward waiting for the corner hit to arrive on your stick. The moment the ball is struck you can feel an opponent bearing down on you at speed and with great strength and control. Her only thought is to stop you from making an effective shot or pass. Surely this puts you under maximum pressure of mind and body. Nothing less than your best performance will suffice.

Should the defending player succeed in intercepting the initial corner hit she can move forcefully with the ball to set up a strong counter-attack. Should she arrive just in time to tackle she has a good chance of winning the ball. If she arrives a fraction too late for the tackle, at least her stick will have to be avoided by the shooting player. Any rushing defender who stops about three strides away from her opponent is asking for trouble. She is not putting pressure on to her opponent, she is creating the possibility of deflecting a shot around her own goalkeeper, and she is presenting her legs as a target for the shot directed at goal. When a shooting attacker has started the downswing of her drive she can do nothing to alter the outcome of events. If the space to goal was there when the attacker started her swing she has every right to shoot and defenders placing themselves in the way are helping nobody. Martyrdom is not the object of the exercise.

Taking the simplest attacking tactic of using four players evenly spaced on the circle edge as a starting point for our defence deliberations we can look at the intention of the defending unit. Normally it deploys one defender to intercept, tackle or mark the stick of each of those attackers. This leaves one defending player to cover the space behind the other four (should a pass be made as in normal midfield play) and the goalkeeper to block the goal. All things being equal it is best that each defender fulfils her normal role and takes her usual opponent. Thus, at a corner (long), the nearer wing half will try to intercept the corner hit by placing herself ball-side of the attacking player in the main position; the nearer back will go to the stick of her own opponent; the centre-half to the stick of the opposing centre-forward; the further wing half to the stick of the other inner, leaving the further wing unmarked. The back farther from the corner hit will move to a covering position to guard the space in case of passes but not intending to intercept shots, and the goalkeeper will move in front of the line to take the most obvious possible shot, namely that from the inner nearer the corner or the centre of the circle. This positioning is normal defensive covering and therefore expects no defender to undertake an unusual role. As far as they are concerned any opposing attacker in the inner or centre-forward position is the inner or centre-forward for the time being.

Having calmly stated that the nearer wing half will go for an interception of the hit at a corner (long), we have not considered the possibility of that halfback following a few yards behind her adjacent back to pressure the opposing inner. For the following reasons we should prefer the wing half to try to intercept in most cases:

(a) The distance the ball has to travel allows for the possibility of interception.

(b) The defending wing half aiming for an interception leaves the opposing player who is striking the corner hit very little margin of error in her placing of the ball.

(c) That same defending wing half is in a very strong position to start a counter-attack should she intercept the ball.

(d) She is still capable of picking up and marking the player striking the corner hit once that hit has been taken.

The picture at a penalty corner (short) is different and will be discussed later.

If the corner hit actually travels to the nearer opposing inner

F

or centre-forward the defenders have done all that is possible to deal with the situation. However, should it succeed in travelling to the distant inner the defenders are presented with a small dilemma. Let us assume that the hit is taken by the opposing left wing and reaches the right inner. In normal midfield defensive play when the ball crosses the middle of the field in this way the defending left back would move to her right inner, the left half to her right wing, the right back would fall into a covering position and the right half would mark the stick of the left inner. When all the play takes place in the close confines of a 16 yd. (14·63 m.) circle there is little time or space for so many changes to take place. Once the opposing right inner has the ball, clearly the right wing, so far left free, has to be marked. Who should do the job? The normal defensive swing could be used but for certain reasons it would take the risk of leaving the opposing right inner in possession free and the right wing free, while the defending left half moved out to her and the left back up to the right inner. At such a time it would seem economical and sound for the left half, already dashing to mark the opposing right inner's stick, to continue in that course and for the covering left back, who has to move anyway, to mark the opposing right wing leaving the defending right back to fall into a covering position while the right half moves on to the opposing left inner. It is not ideal but at least only three defenders have to change their positioning rather than four and the opposing right inner will never have been free. The goalkeeper meanwhile has to be very nimble indeed to place herself nearer to her left-hand goal-post rather than the one on her right. Anticipating such an eventuality, only three of the six defenders have to bear in mind a possible quick alteration of their moves: namely, the two backs and the goalkeeper. The right half has a little more time to alter her run because of the time it takes for the ball to pass from attacking left to right. A determined, knowledgeable, calm defending unit can take this attack in its stride.

When a penalty corner is awarded the defenders are under severe pressure. Their player nearest to the ball is likely to have to run on a diagonal line to her opponent and the ball has to travel a comparatively short distance. Because an interception of the initial corner hit is highly unlikely it might be wise for the wing half to 'hunt in pairs' with her adjacent back who will move like a rocket to her opposing inner. The wing half should follow about 2 yd. (1·83 m.) behind the back ready to effect either of two jobs. Should that inner receive the ball and attempt to dodge the back before shooting, the wing half will be there to make a second tackle. The centre-half will deal with any dodge towards the centre of the field. If the inner takes the ball and tries to pass it to the wing who struck the corner hit, the defending wing half is ready to move laterally to intercept the pass or to tackle the wing should the pass reach her. The distance kept between the back and the halfback as they move to their opponents is vital. If the wing half is too close to the back the dodge which beats the former will also beat the latter. If the wing half is too far from her back or not ready to veer to the outside of the circle, she will not be able to deal with the pass to the corner hitter.

If, as the attacking players are arranging themselves ready to receive a penalty corner hit from the right, the defenders notice the position of the attacking right inner waiting fairly close to the goal-line ready to collect a short diagonal hit, the defending left half might find it sensible to start her run from behind the goal-line exactly where the circle-line meets it. She will be 5 yd. (4·57 m.) from the ball when it is hit. She will not be between her opposing player and the goal but she will have given herself the shortest distance to travel. The risk may well be worth while.

Some teams are known to prefer using a hand-stop at a corner hit. In such cases the defending team would be wise to deploy their fastest player behind the goal-line whether she usually plays a defensive role or not. Somebody has to reach that ball before a shot can be made. If the opposing attacking team clearly indicates its intention of using a hand-stop at the corner hit the defenders have to adapt. The fastest player goes to the receiver closely followed by another defender to offer maximum pressure to the shooting player. In these circumstances it is highly unlikely that any pass will be made by the attacking team. They are staking their chances on a quick shot. It may be that the goalkeeper will feel happier having the back a little in front of the goal-line covering the acute angle for a shot at goal.

Nevertheless at this time the defenders must ensure that they are ready for a 'dummy' on the part of the opponents. The sticks of the attacking players nearest to the apparent recipient must be marked and any apparent space at the crown of the circle must be covered. It is sounder if the defending players undertake their normal roles as nearly as possible so that if the initial shot never materializes each defender habitually reacts by moving into her next position. In this way maximum security is ensured and confusion will be avoided.

On these occasions some defending units feel safer if one back remains just in front of the goal-line between the left-hand side of the goalkeeper and the goal-post. This can be a very effective method of covering the acutely angled shot much favoured from the hand-stop. Alternatively, both backs may choose to remain slightly ahead of the goal-line, each of them covering a corner of the goal-mouth while the goalkeeper moves well ahead of the goal-line to curtail the angle of any shot. The defenders have taken very obvious severe risks. The two backs in the goal-mouth have nothing other than a small piece of wood with which to stop the ball. Should the latter touch any part of the legs or body of the defending player a penalty stroke will be awarded. On the other hand, the ball might be lifted high. The shot might be a scoop or the ball could have been squeezed between the sticks of the shooting player and the defending one aiming to prevent the shot and fly high and fast towards the goal. Though any player is allowed to stop a high ball with a hand, only the goalkeeper is allowed some leeway for the ball which rebounds slightly forward from her hand. Again the award of a penalty stroke might be being risked. The other problem which might arise concerns the position well ahead of the goal-line assumed by the goalkeeper. Supposing the first shot has been stopped by a skilful back who is then swooped upon by the rushing attackers. The goalkeeper is still well away from the line, leaving the one back alone able to use nothing but her stick to cover the large area of goal-mouth. The back has little chance of preventing the ball from being poked into the goal or of intercepting a short pass to be followed by another shot. She cannot be expected to cope with several players positioned between the goalkeeper and herself. None of them can be offside because they are behind the ball and the goalkeeper will find it very difficult to get back closer to her goal-line quickly enough to be of use. In attempting to do so she runs a severe risk of obstructing the attacking players.

In spite of all these risks many continental teams use this tactic very successfully so it is certainly worth considering. So long as attacking players fail to make the most of the advantages offered to them in this ploy, defending units will be justified in using it.

Tactics are as fascinating to the good hockey player as are numbers to the expert mathematician. It seems likely that different methods of probing the solidarity of an opposition will continue to arise during matches, creating new problems, each requiring a new answer or an adaptation of an old response. Consequently, tactical knowledge can never be complete. Players and coaches who retain an alertness to the happenings of the moment and whose minds remain flexible enough to enjoy facing new possibilities are likely to contribute a good deal to the future development of the game.

6. Unorthodox Play

FOR MANY YEARS the 5-3-2-1 system of play was used most regularly by teams and became recognized as 'orthodox' play so that any departures from this system were considered to be 'unorthodox'. Such changes that occurred were originally changes in formations of a transitory nature produced to counter opposing play or initiate less predictable moves with the system still dictating the basic patterns of play. The unpredictability of the game causes unusual movements of players to happen spontaneously. These have to be countered by the opposition with equally irregular ploys on occasion. For instance, in the orthodox system when a right back makes a fast interception just inside her own half of the field and then decides to go on towards goal, prepared to shoot, she is not producing strictly orthodox play. She has transformed herself into a forward and caused her own players to assume unorthodox positions or roles. The five regular forwards either have to shift laterally to make room for her and adjust their own positions to the altered working space allowed them, or one of them has to drop back and take up the role abandoned by the right back. If the latter course of action is taken observers will adjudge the situation as unusual play by the right back, but not unorthodox play by the team. Though the roles of an attacker and defender have been exchanged the group as a whole retains the 5-3-2-1 system and the opposition need not change their play. If the former course of action is taken then the observer will rightly consider the play unorthodox. There will be six players in attack and only five players remaining to support the front line and cover for a possible counter-attack. How those five players position themselves may add to the unorthodoxy of the situation. Three of them might come closer together a few yards behind the attacker in possession, leaving one defender to cover a large expanse of field and the goalkeeper to guard her goal-mouth.

No matter how the team in possession decides to deploy its other five players it must be unorthodox. Meanwhile the opposition has been forced to consider restructuring its defence to cope with six players in attack. By that one spontaneous decision the attacking right back can have caused her team and the opposing team to adopt unorthodox formations momentarily. Immediately this move is completed both teams will resume their usual positions and roles. This kind of adaptation occurs frequently in good games of hockey and one cannot believe there was ever a time when this was not so.

Thus, unorthodox *formations* tend to be transitory, whereas unorthodox *systems* involve a totally different structure which serves as the basis for the organization of tactical play. The choice of system will depend largely upon the players available so that their strengths may be utilized most frequently and their weaknesses protected. Naturally the system played by the opposition may be influential, and if a team can offer more than one system it may be able to counter the play of the opposition more successfully. Certain principles should be considered when devising or choosing a system of play. The attack should have depth and width and should be capable of being developed as quickly and directly as possible. Players should have an equal share of the work-load and the defence must provide security and a springboard from which attacks may be launched. It may be based on man-to-man marking, or space marking, or a combination of both. It can be organized so that each player understands her role within it and is able to support others when necessary. The system should be based on the defence because their play can be structured and disciplined, whereas the attack benefits from a lack of restriction.

Women's hockey seems to have acquired its unorthodox systems from four sources. In some cases patterns have been copied from men's hockey mainly by teams who are coached by men. Some players have adapted formations seen to be successful in other games and applied them to hockey. Others have sat down and thought about the problem as an academic exercise and produced possibilities. A few have noted the results of a spontaneous un-orthodox event occurring during play and then planned a system around the formation that arose to ensure that it could happen regularly. Provided the system that emerges is successful its source is acceptable, but it seeems reasonable to suppose that the last one named is most likely to be effective since the system grew out of the game rather than being superimposed from without.

Arc and Tail

Here is an example of an unorthodox formation that can be turned on and off during the course of a game as the run of play dictates. This method entails starting the game in the usual positional style and waiting until one of the inners receives the ball cleanly with her opponent some distance away. In fact the inner is in undisputed possession. At this point the wing beside her moves in close on one side, the centre-forward closes in on the other side and brings with her the other inner. Each of these four players should be about $1\frac{1}{2}$ yd. ($1\cdot37$ m.) from the other with the attacker in possession being at the peak of a slight arc formed by the four players. The centre-half swoops in about 3 yd. ($2\cdot74$ m.) behind the player with the ball to produce a compact attacking unit. Progress is made by the player in possession sprinting forward briefly and making a short, crisp, square pass, when an opponent threatens to tackle, to any of the other players who, because they are lying behind the player in possession, move on to the ball at speed and repeat the process. It is important that as a player passes the ball she checks her run so that the small arc is retained. Ground can be gained at amazing speed in this fashion provided that each of the participants has the accuracy of ball control required plus the footwork and self-discipline to stop and start suddenly. The reasons for asking the four attackers to snuggle so closely together are quite simple. A short pass is very difficult for the opposition to intercept. At least three of them might be needed to dispossess the attackers and in such close quarters there is no space for a clean interception. After every unsuccessful poke at the elusive ball an opponent will have to turn and reposition for another attempt at intercepting. All of which eats up energy and gives precious extra seconds to the attackers who have no need to turn. Should one of the opposition manage to poke the ball through between two players in the arc the attacking centre-half, who has been moving in support behind whichever player had possession, picks up the loose ball and carefully pops it

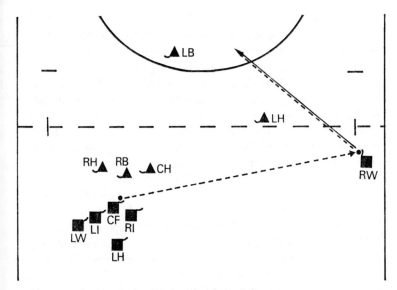

Fig. 7. The arc and tail formation in attack

back to one of the four comprising the arc. No third-party obstruction has taken place because the players in the arc will not attempt to regain possession thus barring the opponents' way and the centre-half has maintained a distance of 3 yd. (2·74 m.) between herself and her own player with the ball. See Fig. 7.

This arc and tail tactic is fun to use. It can be effective in itself, but it is also part of a larger plan of action. The fifth forward, so far ignored, stays well out on the far wing leaving a vast space between herself and the arc; the opposing defenders quite sensibly are drawn towards the massed attack leaving her high and dry. As soon as the opposing defence is fully committed to one side of the field the 'arc' player in possession drives the ball hard into the space ahead of the fifth forward for her to meet it and carry it into the circle for a shot. At the very worst she might have one defender plus the goalkeeper to beat. The play may be switched to the other side of the field too near the half-way line for this glorious long pass to be made. In which case three of the original arc, plus the centre-half, hurtle laterally after the ball to reform the arc.

You might think that no thought has been given to the possibility of an error on the part of the attacking forwards or there being a particularly astute opponent who could foil the plot. Not so. The other members of the attacking team arrange themselves to prevent a quick break by the opposition. The wing half on the side nearer to the play normally positions to prevent a long pass being made to the opposing wing. The back nearer to the play positions slightly to the ball-side of centre, almost as though she were a cautious centre-half, to discourage a cross-pass. The other wing half lies very deep and out to the side to cover another possible line of cross-field pass and support the centre-half comeback. The remaining back plays as a sweeper aligning herself ready to take a long through-pass and the goalkeeper positions herself well away from her goal-line because any counter-attack is likely to be made by a lone forward. If the play switches to the opposite side of the field the more attacking of the two backs acts as the pivot staying fairly central while the other back and the goalkeeper flip like a tail to take up similar positions on the other side of the field. The movement is lateral rather than forward and back. Meanwhile the two wing halves reverse their positioning. This does not claim to be an especially sound defence, but it has covered the most usual routes for quick counter-attacking and it could certainly contain such an attack giving time for the defence to reform on more orthodox lines. By its nature it is plain that this formation is not intended to be sustained throughout a match. It can be very exhausting for the midfield players. Nevertheless it is very useful when it is employed intermittently to force a way through a very sound orthodox opposing defence.

Double Phalanx

An extreme tactic which arose from anticipating the need to defend straight from the bully is worth consideration. The eleven players are arranged in an offset double phalanx down the centre of the field, the centre-forward and the goalkeeper being the two end-pieces with all other players equidistant from each other. In this way two straight lines approximately 2 yd. (1·83 m.) apart are formed parallel to the side-lines. No two players are in line horizontally.

Should the unorthodox team win the bully its players fan out from the double line into orthodox positions to attack as normal. If the opposition win the bully no straight route to goal is open to them so the ball has to be passed to one side or the other. It travels unmolested to inner or wing while the double phalanxes move a comparatively short distance to present two diagonal lines between the middle of the centre-line and the outer edge of the circle on the ball-side of the field. No attempt to tackle is made as the opposition progresses towards the goal until an opponent comes close to the phalanx. This is an adaptation of a tactic used in other games, allowing the attack to build up in order to consolidate a large zone defence near to the shooting area. The particular arrangement of players in this case makes it almost impossible for the ball to cross the field or enter the shooting circle, there being two players blocking each space. Thus the attack has been contained in half the field so the defenders can afford to wait for the ball to be brought close to them.

The moment an opponent with the ball moves close to the phalanx the nearest player from the front line sets off to tackle and harass her. If the defender succeeds a counter-attack is mounted. If the ball is sent to the outside of the field the defender retreats into the line. It is quite possible to send off two defenders in succession to support each other and still maintain a double line by moving the players further along the line down a place.

At the very least two cleverly controlled dodges are needed to penetrate the lines and still there is a goalkeeper with plenty of time and space to anticipate the outcome of the second dodge. Any ball lofted over the lines into the space behind them can also be handled by the mobile goalkeeper and still the pass across is blocked.

When this system is tried opponents may attempt solo dodges; try close stick-to-stick passing near the circle edge; or try passing hard across, hoping the pace of the hit will force a way through. Yet they are rarely successful since even when the defenders mis-field the ball there are so many of them in close proximity able to rectify the mistake and take the ball. Whenever a pass happens to penetrate the double barrier and reach the other side of the field, the defending phalanx only needs to make a small, rapid adjust-ment to present exactly the same wall to the new possessors. When the defending team gains possession it is easy to mount a counter-attack since several players are up the field close to the centre-line,

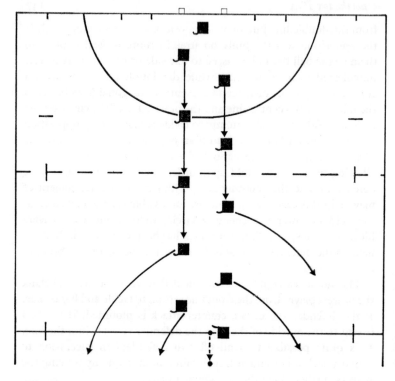

Fig. 8

ready to move to a long pass, knowing the rest of the team will be spreading to give support.

In spite of the success encountered on several occasions by using this system no claim is being made that it is *the* answer. Some big problems came to light. The middle four or five players in the phalanx have a vast amount of ground to cover in order to fan out as wings and halfbacks during the attack and yet re-form the lines when possession is lost. Meanwhile the players at the outer ends of the lines travel much less than would be the case using a normal orthodox pattern. In a match, to avoid overtiring the one group of players it is necessary to change the people forming the middle block. In this case, unless the team comprised ten players versatile enough to play well in any orthodox position, it might well transpire

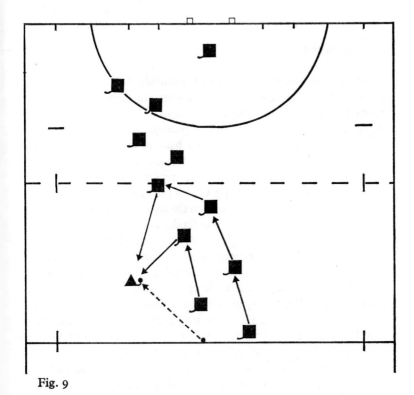

Fig. 9

Figs. 8–9. The double phalanx formation

that no strong striker would be upfield when the moment to attack arose, rendering the plan useless. The severe discipline of moving rapidly into unaccustomed places, resisting the temptation to go to the ball, reading accurately the precise moment to break or re-form the phalanx is difficult to bear. The smallest mistake provides a very good opportunity for the opposition to break through. Opponents realize quickly the improbability of their own players being offside in the circle and capitalize on this. Nevertheless, this formation achieved enough success to prevent its being discarded out of hand. The principles are sound enough. Perhaps there lie within it the roots of a system much more effective than that currently accepted as orthodox.

Zone Defence

When a team committed to attack suddenly loses possession it has to make the most of the few defenders remaining between the counter-attack and its own goal. Using a small part of the tactic just described can be very effective. The principle of preventing opponents from entering the circle is the basis of this simple plan. A zone defence is formed by three defenders plus the goalkeeper. Two of the defenders, keeping about 3 yd. (2·74 m.) apart, plant themselves on the circle edge facing the player in possession. Each is ready to intercept a pass. The one on the stick side of the opponent is also ready to tackle. The third defender is behind the other two, forming the apex of a triangle, ready for a pass between the two front defenders. The goalkeeper is ready to move well away from her goal-line as a double cover should the ball be lifted over the heads of the players forming the triangle or should the ball be missed by the third defender. If play is switched to another part of the circle edge the defending triangle has a comparatively short distance to travel in order to re-form wherever play begins to approach the circle again. The third defender peels off to become one of the front pair nearer the ball while the more distant of the two front defenders moves across to form the apex of the triangle, becoming the new third defender. Even if this minimal defence fails to retrieve possession it can succeed in holding off the opposing attack long enough for the rest of the defence to recover. See Fig. 10.

What possible reasons could there be for deliberately altering a well-tried system? Perhaps the opposition to be faced works with a plan which removes much of the strength of orthodox play. Perhaps they have one or two exceptional forwards who must be closely marked throughout the match. It may be that your own team has a particular strength which the usual system prevents from being used to the full, or a weakness that must be shielded. It may even be that your players are stale and need a radical change to stimulate their thinking and encourage them to read the game more attentively. A team which presents a surprise to its opponents may prevent them from settling into their own style of play quickly and so gain a valuable psychological advantage. Your own team may need to establish firmer control in midfield and be able to disrupt counter-

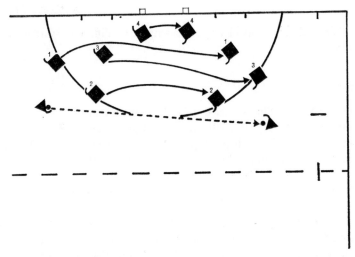

Fig. 10. A zone defence in the circle

attacks earlier, or adopt a formation which protects their own goal-circle and denies entry to the opposition.

Each of these reasons seems to be valid and sensible. Without experiment there can be little progress and it is quite possible that some system at present deemed unorthodox might prove to be better in most circumstances than a system currently accepted as orthodox. The introduction of sweeping new tactics may be particularly effective in breaking a stalemate thereby enabling a team to gain the initiative.

Any team which is too inaccurate, too lacking in skill or stamina to be effective in its normal system of play would be very unwise to assume that adopting a more unorthodox system would solve its problems. It is more than likely to add to them, for unorthodoxy can be very demanding. At its best it requires eleven players each knowing the total game very well indeed—each one, with the exception of the goalkeeper, ready to take on the role of any position as the situation dictates. A very strict discipline has to be maintained or there will be no system, unorthodox or otherwise. Many systems encourage flexibility of role so each player needs to possess the stickwork indigenous to any position found in the game. Most of all, unorthodoxy requires great stamina, determination and concentration, especially in the initial learning stages.

We will now consider some examples of different systems of play.

4-4-2-1

The Defence. This is based on tight man-to-man marking of the four players nearest the ball with the support of two deep covering defenders who by their positioning produce triangular formations. As soon as the opposition gains possession of the ball the four halfbacks identify their opponent and move to mark her. The two deep covering defenders form the apexes of the triangles nearest the ball. See Fig. 11.

The triangular formations are effective in that they restrict the use of through-passes by the opposition and can deal more easily with opposing players who add themselves into the attack. Once the man-to-man marking is established the defenders responsible for the three central attackers never leave their opponent. Thus, what is frequently the most dangerous area of the attack is contained without any positional changes being necessary when the ball moves. Once these basic principles are understood modifications can be prepared to counter possible attacking moves from the opposition. Here are some examples.

If an opponent overlaps between two outside players of an attack (see Fig. 12), then the outer halfback moves off her opponent to tackle the new arrival, i.e. player 1 moves off to tackle player B. Player 4 at the apex of the triangle notes the free lateral attacker and is ready to move to challenge her if she receives a pass. If an opponent overlaps between the three central attackers she is tackled by the apex and the man-to-man marking is retained.

If the opposing team present five regular attackers and the ball is passed to the free player on the far side then the nearest covering back moves across to challenge her. Two further adjustments in the defence are then possible. Firstly, the remaining covering back forms the apex of the triangle between the ball and the goal. Secondly, the halfback furthest from the ball can move off her opponent to cover with the remaining back.

When play is in midfield the two centre halfbacks should avoid playing side by side so that they can control the space for the square-pass or the forward-pass, thereby restricting their oppo-

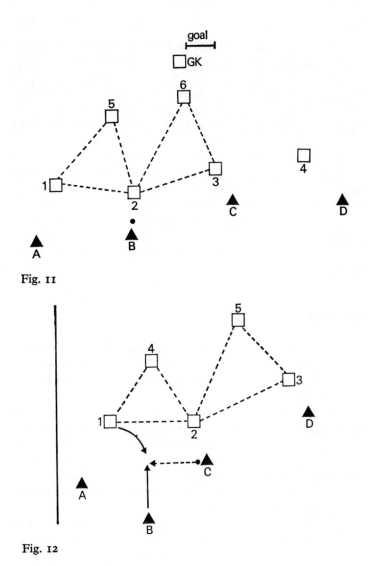

Fig. 11

Fig. 12

Figs. 11–12. Triangular formations

nents' use of the cross-pass. Similarly, the two fullbacks should adjust their positioning to ensure that one is always slightly behind the other and they shift laterally to cover the forward-pass instead of up and back as in the 5–3–2–1 system.

The Attack. The four forwards lead the attack and the two half-backs nearest the ball play in close support producing attacking triangular formations. These offer the opportunity for the support players to receive back-passes, and switch the direction of the attack, add into the attack, overlap the attack and to feed through-passes for the forwards to move on to. At any time the attack can consist of 4 to 8 players and the pressure of play can be maintained.

The 4–4–2–1 system allows a team to establish firmer control of midfield and disrupt opposing attacks earlier than would normally be possible. It restricts the effectiveness of passes played behind the marking defenders because there is always a player lying deep to cover these. It may be counteracted by the opposition using long cross-passes to stretch out the four halfbacks or by the use of a short passing game which causes defenders to commit themselves to the tackle.

3–2–4–1–1

This is a modification of the 5–3–2–1 system in that the two inside forwards drop back behind the front line of the attack and one of the fullbacks joins the line of halfbacks. The remaining fullback acts as a sweeper.

The Defence. The four halfbacks mark the four attackers nearest the ball and the sweeper covers between the ball and the goal. The two inside forwards harass the opposing attackers in midfield and mark any halfback who seeks to add herself into the attack. They also serve as target players to receive passes out of defence and they are responsible for structuring many of the attacks by their skilful distribution of the ball.

The Attack. At least one of the three leading forwards must be capable of evading opponents to go for goal. The others can then play in close support or space out to spread the defence and create openings for penetrating passes. The player with the ball should always be able to choose whether to evade or pass; this is facilitated by the two feeders adding themselves into the attack and offering close support to the player with the ball. This provides some flexibility in attack without detracting from the support which is offered by the four halfbacks.

4-2-4-1

This system, at one time much favoured in soccer, has its devotees and is often thought to be essentially a defensive system though it can provide a springboard for attack.

The Defence. The two halfbacks try to ensure that their opponents cannot feed the ball to the two inside forwards. This can prevent these players from having frequent possession of the ball to initiate attacks, particularly as they are very often the schemers for the team. The four defenders concentrate initially on marking the space in midfield by playing in a diagonal line with the deeper players furthest from the ball. In the circle they switch their attention to man-to-man marking. The two halfbacks add themselves to the line when necessary and each defender marks a space picking up whoever enters her territory. Thus, interchanging by the opposition is rarely effective as the defenders are not tempted to move out of their zone.

The Attack. Support for the attack is weakened in this system because of the work rate demanded of the two halfbacks. Goals tend to be scored from quick counter-attacks and the forwards have to make more effort to tackle back if they lose possession of the ball.

2-3-4-1-1

The Defence. The positioning is based on where the opposition gains possession of the ball. If the opposing left attack has the ball the four halfbacks shift sideways to mark the four players nearest the ball and the furthest of the three link players drops back to mark any player who might be free on the opposing right flank. If there is no free player the link can position to intercept cross-passes. Once all the attackers are marked they stay with the same opponent regardless of the movement of the ball. Each attack player is followed wherever she goes. If the opposing forward line is staggered the defenders deploy as a line just in front of their defending 25 yd. line and pick up their opponent as she approaches. There is a sweeper behind the line to take any through-passes. The weakness of this system is that it involves a lot of running for the outer links, for if the attack starts on the other side the outside link furthest from the ball takes her turn to drop back. If the opposition regains possession in the centre of the field the defenders will have decided in advance which way they will shift. Good anticipation can reduce the energy expended by the outer links and they can also switch positions with other players to share the load. Alternatively five players can constitute the line leaving only two link players. Thus when the opposition plays five forwards the defenders are always responsible for the same opponent unless they have interchanged before the marking is established.

The Attack. When the defence regains possession it feeds the ball to the two remaining links or forwards who move quickly towards goal. It is essential that the attackers can produce a concentrated spearhead attack as well as attacking on a broad front. The two central defenders of the line of four form a defensive triangle with the sweeper at the apex whilst the outer backs support the attack. It is desirable that the two forwards are both capable of evading an opponent.

Blocking the circle is a viable form of defence although we would not encourage its use as it does not reflect the true spirit in which the game should be played. We firmly believe that attack is the best form of defence but in these days when championship points matter it may have its merits and should be considered. When the opposition has the ball six defenders position themselves round the edge of the circle to deny entry to their opponents. Two other players station themselves inside this defensive wall with the goalkeeper and the two remaining players forage outside the circle to harass attackers and regain possession. Playing against this type of defence can be very frustrating as the opponents ignore the ball in midfield and retreat to the circle and once there do not allow themselves to be tempted out of position. In their anxiety to score, the attackers may commit too many players into attack leaving the opportunity for the opposition to break out of defence quickly and score. Attackers may force penalty corners in the crowded conditions providing space and a scoring opportunity, if only momentarily before the opponents beyond the half-way line can return to rejoin their colleagues. Hence the need to develop expertise in the conversion of corners. Moving the ball rapidly and accurately around the edge of the circle may produce an opening or the scoop and flick may be used to penetrate the defensive wall.

At times it may be necessary to suppress the outstanding abilities of an opposing forward by close marking. Where only one forward poses a real threat then two defenders can be given the task of marking her. This can be done by withdrawing a forward to combine with a defender leaving the defensive system intact. When such a forward finds herself shadowed so attentively she may be able to provide space and scoring opportunities for others by drawing her attendants away from the ball or the route to goal. She is likely to wander to try and shake off her opponents and this may cause chaos in her team if they are not ready to adapt to her positioning.

Whatever the system in use there will be occasions in the game when close marking is encountered and frequently this occurs in a two-versus-two situation. Having control of the ball it should be possible for two skilful players to take the ball past two opponents. They have the initiative, the defender has to look for the pass or the dodge, she has to identify deceptive actions and she has to work in co-operation with others in her team to provide the most effective barrier. What are the possibilities open to the players with the ball? They must be able to run off the ball, have that uncanny sixth sense which provides immediate communication with their colleague and have sufficient ball control to carry out their ideas. Presuming these abilities to exist they can co-operate in the following ways:

(a) If the defenders are side by side, as so often occurs with a continental defence, triangular passing cannot be guaranteed to work as the forward pass can be intercepted. So the player with the ball needs to move sideways and place the ball straight through the gap between the two defenders. The sideways movement needs to be very quick and possibly disguised or the defenders will close ranks and the straight pass must have just the right amount of pace to enable the other forward to accelerate on to it and control it without its being intercepted by a covering player or travelling on out of play. Naturally it is easier to place the pass down the non-stick side of the defender. Consideration should be given here to the area in which this takes place. If the attackers are to the left of goal the ball can be sent straight by the right-hand forward down the non-stick side of the defender instead of being placed through the gap. This allows the forward on the left to swoop on to it and continue on a direct route for goal. If play is on the right of the field the original example would probably be more suitable. To save time and aid accuracy of pace and direction the push-pass is likely to be most effective.

(b) The player with the ball can send a short pass towards her colleague who must cut on to it at speed and sweep on with the ball between the two defenders. It may be necessary to move sideways to pull the opponents further apart before executing the pass. The ball must not be given too much pace.

(c) Provided the attacker is a sufficient distance away from the defender she may scoop the ball over her opponent into the forward space for her colleague to collect, but for this to be successful the stroke must not be advertised.

(d) A scissor movement can be effected and obstruction will not occur if the defenders are always allowed a sight of the ball. Thus it works most effectively if the attacker on the right has the ball. She then moves to her left and her colleague passes behind her to collect either a short reverse stick pass or a dead ball. Once the ball is received the second player must accelerate past the defenders choosing her route according to their movements.

These are just four examples of the many choices that are possible and whatever the system in use it can be assumed that players will have to cope with this situation at some time during the game.

Playing any new system demands that players pay more than usual attention to their own positioning and that of other players for patterns of play cannot be predicted as easily as if both teams were playing a more orthodox game. Positioning does not happen as automatically in the early stages and it takes time to become familiar with the situation and meet the different demands which are made. It is good that players should occasionally be shaken out of their complacency and refreshed by the challenge of new ideas. Such an experience quite often has a beneficial effect if players return to their more usual system of play.

The result of a game may often be finely balanced and the smallest incident may be the very thing to tip the balance one way or the other. It takes courage and good training to change to a different, perhaps less familiar system in the middle of a game, but the use of variations may disrupt the opposition sufficiently to provide the brief moment of advantage which can lead to success. A readiness to depart from the orthodox system also allows team selection to be more flexible. It is possible to select the best field players and devise a system to suit their abilities, bearing in mind that some players are more attack-minded, whereas others favour defensive roles. It cannot be said that one system is better than any other. What is important is that the system adopted must suit the players involved and use their abilities to greatest advantage. Used wisely, new formations can be introduced to counter particular patterns of play adopted by known opponents and such methods may be discarded once that game is finished. Tactical systems are only a starting point, providing a structure which helps players to integrate their efforts and a basis from which more fluid patterns of play can evolve. However, any system is only as good as the players who are playing it and if a team is not producing good results a change to a new system will not guarantee greater success. What is important is that players continue to abandon the accepted procedure when necessary and produce those flashes of enterprise and daring which rise above the moment to enrich and enliven the game.

Coaching of Unorthodox Play

This has its own special problems. To the myriad decisions that have to be made by a coach we now have to add that of choosing the best method for ensuring sound mental as well as practical understanding of the new formation. Its aims and purposes must be thoroughly grasped. By the nature of the interdependence of one player on another it is difficult to build such formations gradually or in sections until the whole can be slotted together. Nevertheless, this is what a coach might discover to be the easiest method in the long run. For instance, if the arc and tail ploy is to be used, a group practice of the four close attackers with one ball can be set up to impress the sensation of giving quick, short, square passes and of sprinting forward to receive and carry the ball, then hesitating immediately after passing so that forward progress can be made and yet the player with the ball remains at the peak of the arc. It is very similar in essence to passing in rugby football. Once this unusual stop-start progress has been established the supporting halfback can be added to follow the rapid lateral movement of the ball around the arc. This, too, is an unusual habit for her to acquire.

When a player has the ball her colleagues normally position to receive a pass from her, frequently running at her side. By making a player go for goal with strict instructions not to pass, her team-mates can be persuaded by this single-minded intent to forgo their normal positioning and fall in close behind her. The player with the ball must make every effort to keep going for goal or those around her will be reluctant to relinquish their normal positioning. In this simple way habits have begun to be broken down and new ideas tried. Using small-sided games or opposing groups of unequal numbers could serve the same purpose. Alternatively, the coach can enforce within one team an unusual formation that she knows strains orthodox play giving time for the orthodox team to find its own solution to the problem.

It would be foolish for a coach to superimpose any system on a group of players willy-nilly. Using methods such as those described above, she can remove ingrained responses from players for long enough to give her the opportunity to see their individual and collective spontaneous responses to varying situations as they arise. These vital clues will give the coach a chance to select a system which fits the style of that group of players and which is therefore likely to be adopted more easily. Without such knowledge of the players a coach would run a serious risk of removing one conformity which has lost its appeal to replace it with another which may be alien to that group of players, leaving the team worse off than it was before.

The essential part of this kind of coaching is allowing time for the whole plan to be tried for short spells against realistic opposition. In this way problems of adaptation, difficulties in the understanding of individual players and weaknesses in the system have an opportunity to arise. These can then be dealt with during short talking sessions or by reconstructing moves at a slower pace in between bouts of playing.

There will always be a need for unorthodox behaviour in the game of hockey. For as long as there are courageous players capable of constructive, independent thought we shall continue to see new moves, new formations on a large or a small scale at all levels of play. Trial and error remains the best way of achieving a sense of perspective. Experiments balance between established tactics and new ideas and direct their energy and enthusiasm towards a growing game, thereby injecting some extra sparkle into it.

7. On Reflection

COACHING IS HARD work but it is fun. Indeed it is almost as stimulating as playing and brings nearly as much reward in the form of delight. Whereas the player experiences the game the coach has the satisfaction of seeing a good game well played due in some measure to her own efforts. Though this gives pleasure, at the same time it engenders the desire to improve the game even more. Coaches are sometimes described as meddlers who cannot leave well alone and perhaps this is true to a point; but they can only influence those who are willing to accept suggestions. If we believe that individuals should be given the opportunity to reach their full potential we accept the need for coaching in some form. Many people will never realize their own latent talent without prodding or tuition. This is as true in the sphere of hockey as in any other.

Undoubtedly the coach will influence those she meets and through them the game they play. The same is true of those who deal with administration, who select or who umpire. All of them ultimately affect the game. The coach has an opportunity for sharing her enthusiasm, her aesthetic appreciation together with the knowledge she has amassed through years of experience. In these days of increasing gamesmanship a coach who believes that a game can only take place when opponents agree to respect the same rules by striving not to break them is sorely needed. In such a climate the art of playing hockey can flourish. The game exists in its present form because of the structure of the current rules and must be played within their bounds. This is the challenge that a good coach will place before her pupils. When rules are deliberately and persistently broken the inference is that the players lack sufficient skill to meet the challenge or that they are playing some other nameless game. The coach is in an ideal position to foster such a positive attitude to playing. Though this may be out of fashion, without it the game as we know it cannot survive.

The relationship of players and coach is of great importance. The former must be prepared to discriminate between advice which is of use and that which is not after giving it a fair trial. Both the coach, with her knowledge of the game, and the players must be prepared to face new problems and present new suggestions to stimulate the thinking and skill of those in her charge. Good players expect to have a high work rate demanded of them but they also expect to be given the opportunity of using their initiative and inventiveness. In this way every player will be encouraged to use the last ounce of her ability and so produce a better game.

Administrators, selectors, umpires and coaches strive in their own ways to feed into the game their knowledge, experience and ideas so that it shall continue to exude mental and physical vitality. They intend that the playing of hockey shall be a worthwhile experience.

Ultimately the quality of the game will always be determined by the players. Each one should strive to make the most of her own ability not only in order to achieve maximum fulfilment of her personal talent but also to ensure that the game shall retain its excellence. The spectacle of a good game played by those who enjoy trying to overcome the challenges presented in hockey is a source of inspiration to future devotees. Players have a tremendous responsibility which they should be happy to accept. They set the attitudes and levels of expertise for aspiring players. They provide the majority of future coaches, umpires, selectors and officials. Surely these objectives are worthy of hard work especially as it is accompanied by personal satisfaction at all levels of performance. On reflection, hockey is a rewarding experience.

Index

CAMROSE LUTHERAN COLLEGE
LIBRARY
GV
1017
H7
R4
21,683